# Flavours of
# INDIAN
# COOKING

SNAB
Excellence in Books

# Nita Mehta's™

# Flavours of
# INDIAN
# COOKING

## Nita Mehta

B.Sc. (Home Science), M.Sc. (Food and Nutrition), Gold Medalist

SNAB
Excellence in Books

# Flavours of
# INDIAN
# COOKING

Snab Publishers Pvt Ltd

Corporate Office
3A/3, Asaf Ali Road, New Delhi 110 002
Phone: +91 11 2325 2948, 2325 0091
Telefax: +91 11 2325 0091
E-mail: nitamehta@nitamehta.com
Website: www.nitamehta.com

Editorial and Marketing office
E-159, Greater Kailash II, New Delhi 110 048

Food Styling and Photography by Snab
Typesetting by National Information Technology Academy
3A/3, Asaf Ali Road, New Delhi 110 002

Recipe Development & Testing:
Nita Mehta Foods - R & D Centre
3A/3, Asaf Ali Road, New Delhi - 110002

ISBN 978-81-86004-80-7

6th Print 2013

Cover Designed by:

Printed in India at Infinity Advertising Services (P) Ltd, New Delhi

Price: Rs. 595/-   US$ 29.95   UK£ 20.95

Distributed by :
NITA MEHTA BOOKS
3A/3, Asaf Ali Road, New Delhi - 02
Distribution Centre :
D16/1, Okhla Industrial Area, Phase-I,
New Delhi - 110020
Tel.: 26813199, 26813200
E-mail: nitamehta.mehta@gmail.com
Contributing Writers :
Anurag Mehta
Tanya Mehta
Subhash Mehta
Editors :
Sangeeta
Sunita

## Introduction

The true art of Indian cooking lies in the subtle use and variation of spices which make each dish exotic and an exciting new experience. The use of spices, however, does not mean their use in vast amounts, nor does it mean that all Indian food is extremely hot and spicy, as many people believe. The dishes can be as hot or as mild as the individual family chooses, since this is a matter of personal taste. The best Indian dishes are a clever blend of exotic spices, delicate herbs and vegetables or meat.

Generally, an Indian meal consists of a vegetable dish; a pulse or a non vegetarian dish of either fish, mutton or chicken; a yogurt dish, eaten with bread and/or rice. The vegetable or the non vegetarian dish may be a wet curry or a dry one. Indians use bread to scoop up curries while eating. The meal is usually rounded off with a sweet dish or some fresh fruit.

I am sure you will find this cookbook adventurous and exciting. Look forward to wonderful Indian food and share it with those you love and care about!

Nita Mehta

# CONTENTS

## Drinks & Snacks 31

## Tandoori & Kadhai – Vegetarian 73

## Vegetarian—Curries 59

## Legumes & Pulses 95

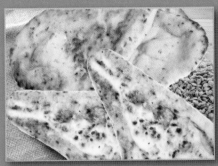

## Chicken & Mutton   105

## Rice & Breads   129

## Desserts & Sweets   153

## Fish & Sea Food   119

## Chutneys & Pickles – Raitas & Salads   143

## Kesar

SAFFRON...Kesar, zaffran, crocus, by whatever name, this golden spice has evoked an aura of romance, richness and rarity through the ages. In India, saffron is worth its weight in gold, its vibrant colour and heady bouquet making it pure ambrosia.

In India it only grows in Pampore in the valley of Kashmir and Kishtwar in Jammu.

Saffron enhances savoury food as well as sweet. A few strands soaked in a little warm water or milk and added along with the liquid to the dish adds a fragrant richness. Even the most simple dish can be transformed into something magical by the addition of saffron.

# Haldi

TURMERIC...One of the most traditional and versatile of spices used in Indian cooking, turmeric is the very heart and soul of any curry. This key ingredient is used daily in every part of India as its unique colour and flavour enriches every regional cuisine.

It has also been used for centuries as a curative and cleansing agent. Since early times, it has been associated with purification so that even today, an Indian bride and groom are ritually anointed with turmeric as part of a cleansing ceremony.

Turmeric is stored in every Indian house - its use as a quick antiseptic, as a beauty aid and, of course, as a versatile cooking spice makes this condiment a truly exceptional part of the traditional Indian spice box.

# Lal Mirch

RED CHILLI...Indian food without chillies is like summer without sunshine, that is not to say that all Indian food scorches the taste buds, rather that it is an amicable blend of heat, fragrance and flavour.

Chillies actually cool down the system in hot weather. The capsaicin dilates blood vessels to increase circulation and encourage perspiration. However, if you do suffer, don't reach for a jug of water - capsaicin is insoluble in water (like oil). Dairy products have the power to neutralise capsaicin so try yoghurt, or milk to douse the fire.

The pungency can vary from the mild Kashmir chilli to the dried south Indian varieties which have incredible firepower. As with all ground spices, chilli powder loses its strength and sparkle after a few months.

# Dhaniya

DRY CORIANDER...The seeds which constitute the spice are round and have fine, longitudinal ridges.

They have a sweet, heady aroma with a subtle whiff of pine and pepper.

Make your own coriander seeds powder in a mortar or food processor after dry-roasting. It is fresh, unadulterated and considerably more fragrant than ready-made. Suited to almost every Indian savoury dish, it is an essential part of the Indian spice box.

Besides the flavour, it thickens curries and chutneys. Coriander seeds are said to be diuretic, antibilious, and carminative.

# Garam Masala

Each region of India has its own special spice blend, depending on availability, climate and methods of cooking. In the north, where the winters are bitterly cold, a blend called garam masala, meaning hot spice, is preferred to chillies which cool the body by promoting perspiration. Some of the most expensive spices go into the making of garam masala and there are as many recipes for it as there are households in India. The basic blend includes cloves, cinnamon, cardamom, peppercorns, bay leaf, mace, cumin and coriander seeds. When ground, the powder is slightly coarse and tobacco-brown in colour.

Indian cooks use garam masala in small amounts. It can be added at different stages of cooking for different degrees of flavour. It can be dropped into hot oil to give a spicy, fried taste, added along with the main ingredient to create an aromatic warmth, or sprinkled on top of curries or yoghurt for a gentle hint of spicy flavour.

# Jeera

CUMIN..This gentle spice can be tasted in the rich meat curries of northern Kashmir and in the coconut curries of the south, the exquisite vegetarian fare of Gujarat as well as in the river fish preparations of Bengal.

They range from sage-green to tobacco-brown in colour and have longitudinal ridges.

In India most curries start off with a loud crackle as cumin seeds hit the hot oil, before the meat or vegetables are added. It is not at all difficult to make cumin powder at home. Roast the seeds on a griddle until they change colour and crush them into a fine toasty powder. Roasting the cumin releases and enriches its earthy flavour. Store cumin in a dry place away from light. The powder must be used within 3 months.

Roasted cumin powder is sprinkled on top of salads or yoghurt as a dark, contrasting, aromatic garnish.

# Chhoti Elaichi

CARDAMOM...One of the most popular spices in the world, cardamom is called the 'queen of spices', second only to black pepper, the king. The Mughal emperors of India carried tiny silver boxes of cardamom pods which were chewed as a mouth freshener, a tradition that exists even today amongst the rich and famous of the country.

They are oval capsules containing between 10 to 40 hard, dark brown seeds that are sticky and cling together. Whole cardamom seeds have a sweet flavour and a mild, pleasant aroma. As soon as they are crushed, they release a strong, camphorous fragrance and if chewed, the taste is bittersweet, aromatic and lingering.

Indian savouries and sweets are both flavoured with cardamom. This fragrant spice is used in rich, red curries and milky desserts. In India tea is often spiked with cardamom.

## Sarson

MUSTARD...It is believed to possess the ability to calm the mind, create a peaceful personality and sharpen intelligence. There are 3 main varieties of mustard: brown, black and yellow.

Raw mustard seeds have almost no smell, but on cooking, they acquire a distinctive, acrid, baked-earth aroma that dominates any dish. The seeds are sharp, nutty, slightly bitter and aromatic in taste. Mustard paste has a unique flavour that hits you in the nose and then sings in your veins!

In the south of India and along the coast, mustard is used primarily in the tempering or baghar of spices. This simple procedure of heating oil until very hot, dropping in the mustard seeds and cooking them until they pop and crackle, gives many dishes a distinctive flavour. In Bengal, mustard seeds are crushed to a paste for use in fiery marinades and curries. Mustard is an excellent preservative and split seeds, which look like tiny lentils, are widely used for pickling.

# Chakri phool

STAR ANISE...One of the most beautiful spices available. It lends its delicate fragrance to north Indian dishes.

Dried star anise is mahogany in colour, hard and has eight hollow, boat-shaped petals which form a perfect star. Each point of the star contains shiny, bead-like, oval seeds. Though star anise is not related to aniseed, the spice is similar in flavour, but the aromatic, sweet taste is more pronounced.

In India it is almost always sold whole though in other countries it is available ground or broken into pieces. Being dried and whole, it keeps well for up to a year.

In India, it is used mainly in rice dishes like biryani and in succulent meat curries. Star anise is considered an exotic spice and its addition to any food makes the dish slightly more special!

# Whole Spices

These release their flavour when put in hot oil. The most common whole spices used in Indian cooking are cinnamon, cloves, black cardamom and peppercorns.

Cinnamon: It is the dried inner bark of the tree. The taste is warm, sharply sweet and aromatic.

Black cardamom: It is used only in savouries, especially in rice dishes like biryani.

Cloves: The flavour is so powerful that if too many cloves are used, the other flavours in the dish are completely lost, so they must, be used carefully.

Peppercorns: The most commonly used pepper is round, black, shrivelled and hard. The taste of pepper is just spicy hot. The aroma is woody, penetrating, pungent and aromatic and is good enough to rustle up a healthy appetite.

# Other Herbs, Spices & Ingredients

Used For Flavouring Indian Dishes

The Indian names have been given in italics within brackets.

 **Asafoetida (Hing) :** This pungent, almost unpleasant smelling spice is a resinous gum that is available in it's lumpy and ground forms. It is used in very small amounts in a dish and sautéed in oil before adding the other ingredients. It imparts a pleasant flavour to the cooked dish and also aids digestion.

 **Bay Leaves (Tej patta) :** These fragrant leaves with pointed ends are used in their dried form. These are used in curries and rice preparations.

 **Cardamom Pods (Elaichi) :** This spice is native to India, where it is considered to be the most prized spice after saffron. The pods can be used whole or the husk can be removed to release the seeds. These have a sharp initial bite that soon mellows into a delicate and refreshing fragrance. There are two types of cardamom pods available in India, the small green (chhoti or hari elaichi) and the larger black ones (bari or moti elaichi).

 **Carom Seeds (Ajwain) :** These are tiny purple-brown seeds which look like celery seeds but are slightly pungent. When crushed, they release a strong and lightly aromatic, thyme like fragrance, but on cooking the flavour becomes milder.

 **Cinnamon (Dalchini) :** The true cinnamon has tightly rolled tubular sticks. This Indian cinnamon has thicker flattish sticks. Cinnamon has a delicate, sweet aroma.

 **Cloves (Laung) :** These dried unopened flower buds have a sharp pungent and almost bitter taste. These are used in vegetables & rice pulaos.

**Coriander Seeds (Saboot dhaniya) :** These are small, ribbed and spherical seeds. When lightly roasted & crushed, these add a wonderful flavour to the cooked dishes.

**Coriander Seeds, Ground (Dhaniya powder) :** Coriander seeds are ground to a fine powder. This is an important constituent of most curries. It helps in thickening curries.

**Coriander, Fresh (Hara dhaniya) :** Fresh green coriander is a fragrant herb which is used both in cooking and sprinkled over dishes as an attractive garnish. The green stalks are full of flavour and so the stalks should also be finely chopped along with the leaves and used in flavouring dishes.

**Cumin Seeds, Black (Shah jeera) :** These fine, slender seeds of shah jeera are darker in colour and therefore also referred to as black cumin. These are used for flavouring curries and rice.

**Cumin Seeds, White (Jeera) :** These are one of the most important spice seeds in Indian cooking. These are pale brown, oval seeds which have a strong aroma. These can be used whole or ground. The roasted seeds when ground, lend a delicious flavour to yogurt.

**Curry Leaves (Kari patta) :** These are used mostly in South Indian cooking. They are available fresh or dried. Most Indian homes grow a young plant in a pot, so as to get maximum flavour from the fresh leaves.

**Dill (Soya) :** It is an annual or biennial herbaceous plant with silky, wispy leaves, clusters of small yellow flowers and oval, flattened fruits. The green herb with its unique, fresh taste is a versatile kitchen plant and goes beautifully with fish, yoghurt, meats salads and lentils.

# Other Herbs, Spices & Ingredients (continued...)

 **Fennel (Saunf) :** These oval, yellowish green seeds are similar in appearance to cumin seeds. They have a sweetish taste and are used to flavour rice dishes (biryanis), curries and pickles.

 **Fenugreek Greens, Dried (Kasoori methi) :** The fresh greens of the fenugreek plant are dried and used to flavour both, curries and dry dishes.

 **Fenugreek Seeds (Methi dana) :** These are flat, oblong, mustard brownish seeds. Although these have a slight bitter taste, when raw, but when cooked right, enhance the flavour greatly in vegetables and curries. Always use them in small amounts.

 **Garam Masala :** This is a mixture of spices which can be made by grinding whole spices in a coffee grinder, or purchased ready made from Indian stores. A typical mixture includes cumin seeds, peppercorns, cloves, cinnamon & black cardamom pods. The recipe to prepare garam masala at home is given on page 29.

 **Garlic (Lahsun) :** This is a standard ingredient, along with ginger, in most curries. It is crushed, chopped or used as a paste in Indian cooking. Bottled garlic paste is also available. When crushed, 6-8 flakes of fresh garlic are equivalent to 1 tsp of garlic paste.

 **Ginger (Adrak) :** One of the most important ingredient in many curries. 1 inch/2.5 cm piece of ginger is equivalent to 1 tablespoon of minced ginger. Bottled ginger pastes are also available.

 **Green chillies (Hari mirch) :** These may be very hot, although there are some varieties which are very mild. Generally, the smaller the chilli, the hotter it is. Always remember to wash hands after chopping them. If the seeds are removed, the heat lessens, so I normally deseed the chillies first and then chop them for my recipes.

**Holy Basil (Tulsi) :** Holy basil is considered one of the most sacred plant of India. It is an integral part of Hindu ceremonies and sacraments. The whole plant has a green, woodland perfume and the leaves taste peppery, almost like a cross between ginger and mint. Tulsi tea is quite popular in India.

**Mace (Javitri) :** This is the lacy covering of the seed of the nutmeg tree. It has a rich, warm fragrance and a sweet flavour. Indians use it sparingly, adding it to only rich and creamy dishes. Mostly it is added to various spice blends.

**Mango Powder (Amchoor) :** Raw mangoes are sun dried and ground to a fine powder. This fine powder is used as a souring agent instead of lemon juice in cooked dishes. It is also used in the preparation of various drinks, chutneys and spice blends.

**Melon Seeds (Magaz) :** These are shelled seeds of melons. It makes the Indian curries thick, rich and flavourful. It is also added to drinks and desserts.

**Mint (Poodina) :** A fragrant herb used in Indian cooking. Only the leaves are used. Mint is mostly added to biryanis (Moghul rice preparation), lassi – the North Indian refreshing drink and is also used for making a spicy chutney in combination with coriander.

**Mustard Seeds (Rai, Sarson) :** These may be reddish brown or blackish in colour. Indian cuisine generally makes uses of the dark variety. They have a sharp, pungent flavour which mellows after they are cooked in hot oil or dry roasted. The Southern part of India uses mustard to flavour almost all their dishes.

# Other Herbs, Spices & Ingredients (continued...)

 **Nigella Seeds (Kalaunji) :** These are charcoal black triangular seeds, resembling onion seeds, and are often mistakenly referred to as such. These have a mild flavour, which enhances when added to baked flat breads (naan and roti). Also used in pickles.

 **Nutmeg (Jaiphal) :** It is the oval, brown kernel of the seed of the nutmeg tree. It has a rich warm fragrance and a sweet antiseptic flavour. It is used in various spice blends.

 **Peppercorns (Saboot kali mirch) :** Ground or crushed black peppercorns add a delectable taste to soups, salads and main dishes. These are even used whole in the preparation of vegetables and rice dishes like pulaos.

 **Pomegranate Seeds, Dried (Anardana) :** These are the sun-dried seeds of sour pomegranates. The flesh around the seeds dries and forms a brown-black sticky coating on the seed. These seeds have a predominantly sour taste, yet there is a latent sweetness in them. They are available in their whole or ground form and are used in various chutneys and bean dishes. When they are ground and dry-roasted, they impart a rich brown colour and a welcome tanginess to various chutneys.

 **Poppy Seeds (Khus-khus) :** These seeds are very tiny and light ivory to beige in colour. When cooked they have a distinct nutty aroma. Their graininess is often used to give texture to Indian dishes. In India, poppy seeds are usually ground with other spices and used to thicken curries for meat, fish and vegetables.

 **Red Chilli Powder (Lal mirch) :** This fiery ground spice should be used with caution. The heat varies from brand to brand, so adjust quantities to suit your taste buds. Paprika or Degi mirch may be substituted if you do not want the dish to be hot.

**Red Peppers, Dried (Sukhi lal mirch) :** These provide spicy hot flavour to foods. If you want to make your dishes milder, break the stem and tap gently to discard seeds. These are used in many savoury dishes. You may leave them or remove them before serving a dish.

**Rock Salt (Kala namak) :** This salt is procured from the earth and not the sea. It is also called black salt or saindhav. Rock salt is mined from the soft-stone quarries of the fertile Gangetic plains in central India. Rock salt has a peculiar, unpleasant aroma and a salty taste that is less powerful than common salt. The strange flavour seems to acquire a personality when added to street food snacks, chaat and yogurt delicacies. The one flavour that all these snacks rely on for their zip is of kala namak or rock salt.

**Saffron (Kesar) :** The dried strands of the saffron crocus, is used to colour & flavour a dish, whether sweet or savoury. Saffron is sold as strands. It has a lovely flavour & aroma. The strands should be soaked in a little warm milk or water for 10-12 minutes and then added to the dish being cooked, to impart all of it's flavour.

**Star Anise (Chakri phool) :** Dried star anise is mahogany in colour, hard and has eight hollow, boat-shaped petals which form a perfect star. Each point of the star contains shiny, bead-like, oval seeds. Though star anise is not related to aniseed, the spice is similar in flavour, but the aromatic, sweet taste is more pronounced.

**Sesame Seeds (Til) :** These small, teardrop-shaped, flat seeds are quite tasteless in their raw state but impart a wonderful nutty flavour after roasting. These range from cream to black in colour. The taste and visual appeal of baked or fried food is greatly enhanced, when they are coated with sesame seeds.

**Turmeric (Haldi) :** This bright yellow, bitter tasting spice is sold ground. It is used mainly for colour rather than flavour. It has great antiseptic properties too.

1. Kokum
2. Methi Dana
3. Degi Mirch
4. Sabut Dhania
5. Haldi
6. Kasuri Methi
7. Lal Mirch Powder
8. Sabut Safed Mirch
9. Dhania Powder
10. Sukhe Matar
11. Dalchini
12. Javitri
13. Chhoti Elaichi
14. Chakri Phool
15. Sukhi Lal Mirch
16. Moti Elaichi
17. Laung
18. Kesar

Hing

Til

4

5

6

7

8

9

10

11

12

13

Sabut Kali Mirch

Tej patta

Jaiphal

Jeera

Rai / Sarson

Amchoor

Shah Jeera

Magaz

Chaat Masala

Ajwain

Garam Masala

# Paneer Cheese

*Makes 250 g/8 oz or about thirty, 1 inch/2.5 cm square pieces, ¼ inch/6 mm thick*

*Paneer is a type of fresh cheese prepared by curdling milk and then separating the curds from the whey by passing everything through a fine cheese cloth. The cheese (paneer) remains in the cloth and the liquid whey drains out. For making Indian paneer cheese, nonfat milk does not work well because the cheese prepared from it is tough and chewy. 2 percent low fat milk may be used but full cream milk gives the softest paneer. The milk is curdled with a souring agent after the milk actually boils. Nonfat plain yogurt is the best choice as the souring agent because it makes the best tasting paneer with no extra flavour added to it. Lemon juice may also be used. White vinegar imparts a distinct flavour to the paneer which has to be camouflaged with spices. The basic recipe to prepare paneer cheese is given below.*

## Basic Recipe of Paneer Cheese

### INGREDIENTS

- 1.25 kg/1 quart (2 pints) full fat milk
- 1 cup plain yogurt - whisked
- 4 layers of cheese cloth or 1½ feet/45 cm square piece of fine muslin cloth

### METHOD

1. Rinse a large, heavy bottomed sauce pan. Place the milk in it. Boil milk, stirring continuously to prevent skin forming at the top. When it comes to a boil, reduce heat and immediately add yogurt. Return to high heat, stir gently, till all the milk curdles and the greenish water called whey separates.

2. Remove from heat. Leave it covered for 5 minutes. Firm curds will form.

3. Strain through a muslin cloth placed over a large, deep bowl, tie the ends together and let it hang for at least 30 minutes, then press to squeeze out all the whey. (This whey is valued as a cool drink, and often used in the treatment of stomach upsets.) The paneer cheese remains in the cloth. If cubes of paneer cheese are required, twist the cloth gently and place between two flat plates and place a heavy object like a pan of water on it for 10-15 minutes. Remove the heavy object and let the cheese cool down.

4. Cut into desired shape.

## Baked Ricotta Cheese as a substitute for paneer

*You can get something very similar to paneer cheese by baking ricotta cheese in the oven at 350°F/180°C for about 30 minutes. The water dries out and the solid mass can be cut into cubes, tasting very much like paneer cheese. Cut the baked ricotta into cubes after it cools down a little. Use it in the recipes instead of paneer. Paneer can even be substituted with tofu, prepared from soya bean milk, although the flavour is quite different.*

# Garam Masala

*Makes ¼ cup*

## INGREDIENTS

- 5-6 long sticks cinnamon (dalchini); 15-20 black cardamom pods (moti elaichi); 3/4 tbsp cloves (laung); 2 tbsp black peppercorns (saboot kali mirch); 2 tbsp cumin seeds (jeera); ½ flower of mace (javitri)

## METHOD

1. Remove seeds of black cardamoms. Discard skin.

2. Roast all ingredients together in a pan for 2 minutes on low heat, stirring constantly, till fragrant.

3. Remove from heat. Cool. Grind to a fine powder in a clean coffee or spice grinder. Store in a small jar with a tight fitting lid.

# Sambhar Masala

*Makes ½ cup*

## INGREDIENTS

- ¼ cup coriander seeds (saboot dhania); 1 tbsp cumin seeds (jeera); 1 tbsp dried, split yellow chick peas (channe ki dal); 2 tsp fenugreek seeds (methi daana); 5-6 dry, red chillies (saboot lal mirch); ½ tsp asafoetida (hing); 1½ tsp peppercorns (saboot kali mirch)

## METHOD

1. Roast all ingredients together over low heat in a pan, until fragrant.

2. Cool the spices and grind to a fine powder in a small coffee grinder. Store in an air tight jar.

# Tandoori Masala

*Makes ½ cup*

## INGREDIENTS

- 2 tbsp coriander seeds (saboot dhania); 2 tbsp cumin seeds (jeera); 1 tbsp fenugreek seeds (methi daana); 1 tbsp black peppercorns (saboot kali mirch); 1 tbsp cloves (laung); seeds of 8 black cardamom pods; (moti elaichi); 2 tsp degi mirch; 1 tbsp dried fenugreek leaves (kasoori methi); 1 tbsp ground cinnamon (dalchini); ½ tbsp ground ginger (sonth); ½ tsp red chilli powder

## METHOD

1. In a pan, roast together - coriander seeds, cumin seeds, fenugreek seeds, black pepper corns, cloves and cardamom seeds, on moderate heat for about 1 minute, until fragrant.

2. Remove from heat and let the spices cool down. Grind to a fine powder. Transfer to a bowl and mix in the remaining ingredients. Store in an air tight jar.

# Chaat Masala

*Makes 3/4 cup*

## INGREDIENTS

- 3 tbsp cumin seeds (jeera); 1 tbsp ground ginger (sonth); 2 tsp carom seeds (ajwain); 2 tsp raw mango powder (amchoor); 2 tbsp ground, black salt (kala namak); 1 tsp salt; 1 tsp ground black pepper; ½ tsp ground nutmeg (jaiphal)

## METHOD

1. Roast cumin seeds in a small pan or a kadhai to a golden brown colour. Transfer to a bowl and set aside.

2. Roast carom seeds over moderate heat for about 2 minutes, till fragrant.

3. Grind roasted cumin seeds and carom seeds. Mix in the remaining ingredients.

4. Store in an air tight jar.

# DRINKS & SNACKS

Indian drinks have specially chosen spices which promote the appetite and also aid digestion. These can be served just before a meal as an appetizer or can be taken along with the main meal. The snacks and finger foods included, make an ideal start to the meal, or can be enjoyed as tea time snacks. Serve them with a cool yogurt - cucumber dip or with a spicy mint chutney.

# TOMATO RASAM

*Serves 6-8*

*An authentic, thin tomato soup of southern India, delicious as an appetizer.*

## INGREDIENTS

- 1 kg/2 lb tomatoes - cut into 4 pieces
- 3 cups water
- 1 tbsp oil
- 2-3 whole, dry, red chillies
- 1 tsp cumin seeds *(jeera)*
- 1 tsp mustard seeds *(rai)*
- ¼ tsp asafoetida *(hing)*
- a few curry leaves
- ¼ tsp ground turmeric *(haldi)*
- 1½ tsp salt, or to taste
- 1½ tsp peppercorns *(saboot kali mirch)*
- 1 small pod garlic, whole

## METHOD

1. Boil whole tomatoes with 3 cups water, keep on low heat for about 10 minutes, till tomatoes turn soft. Remove from heat and cool. Blend to a puree.

2. Heat 1 tbsp oil. Reduce heat and fry the red chillies till they turn a shade darker. Add together - cumin seeds, mustard seeds and asafoetida. When cumin turns golden, add curry leaves.

3. Add the pureed tomatoes. Add salt and ground turmeric. Separate the flakes of garlic from the pod and crush them roughly without peeling the flakes. Separately, crush or pound the peppercorns too. Add the crushed garlic and peppercorns to the tomatoes. Boil. Simmer for 10 minutes. Remove from heat.

4. Strain. Discard the ingredients in the strainer. Serve soup garnished with coriander leaves.

Step 4

**NUTRITIONAL VALUES** (per portion): Energy 43.13 cal, Protein 1.75gm, Carbohydrate 4.25 gm, Fat 2.00 gm

# THANDAI

*A festive drink prepared from nuts and flavourful spices blended in milk.*

## INGREDIENTS

- 6 cups of milk
- 1½ cups almonds
- 2 tbsp cashews - broken into bits
- 1/3 cup seeds of watermelon (*magaz*)
- 8 tsp poppy seeds (*khus khus*)
- 15-20 peppercorns (*saboot kali mirch*)
- 10-12 green cardamoms (*chhoti elaichi*)
- 1 tbsp dried rose petals
- 2 tsp fennel seeds (*saunf*)
- 10 tbsp sugar or rose syrup
- a few strands of saffron (*kesar*) - soaked in 1 tsp water for garnishing

## METHOD

1. Soak almonds separately in water for 3-4 hours. Peel almonds. Soak together — watermelon seeds, poppy seeds, cashews, peppercorns, cardamoms, rose petals and fennel seeds for 3-4 hours. Strain.

2. Add the peeled almonds to the strained ingredients. Put all the soaked ingredients in a mixer grinder and grind to a paste by adding a little water or milk. The grinding of the ingredients should be done very well. Grind well to a smooth paste.

3. Add the ground ingredients to the cold milk. Add sugar or rose syrup and mix well. Strain the milk through a cheese cloth and discard the residue.

4. Chill the drink by adding ice. Serve garnished with soaked saffron strands and fresh rose petals.

Step 1

**NUTRITIONAL VALUES** (per portion): Energy 89.43 cal, Protein 5.60 gm, Carbohydrate 4.33 gm, Fat 4.37 gm

# MINTY MUSHROOM ROLLS

*Serves 8-10*

*Mushrooms cooked in butter and flavoured with mint, are stuffed into boiled potato cases and deep fried to a rich brown colour. The bread added to the potatoes makes it crisp and easy to handle.*

## INGREDIENTS

- 4 boiled potatoes - mashed or grated (2 cups)
- 2 slices of bread - ground in a mixer to get fresh crumbs
- ½ tsp garam masala
- ½ tsp red chilli powder
- salt to taste
- oil for frying
- egg white and bread crumbs to coat

### FILLING

- 1 tbsp butter
- 150 g/5 oz mushrooms - chopped (1½ cups)
- ¼ cup finely chopped mint leaves
- 1 large onion - chopped (½ cup)
- salt and pepper to taste

## METHOD

1. Boil potatoes. Mash well while still hot or grate them if they have turned cold. To the mashed potatoes, add fresh bread crumbs, garam masala, red chilli powder and salt to taste. Keep aside.

2. To prepare the filling, heat butter in a pan. Add onions and cook till soft. Add mushrooms. Sauté for 3-4 minutes and let them turn dry. Add mint, salt and pepper to taste. Mix well. Remove from heat.

3. Divide the potato mixture into 8 balls. Flatten each potato ball to a diameter of about 3 inch/8 cm. Place 1 tbsp of mushroom and mint filling on it. Press. Cover the filling by lifting the sides of the potato. Shape into a roll. Flatten the sides of the roll.

4. Beat egg white lightly with 1 tbsp water. Dip the roll in egg white and then roll over bread crumbs to coat.

5. Heat oil in a pan and fry till golden brown. Serve with tomato ketchup or mint or hari chutney as given on page 146.

Step 1

Step 4

**NUTRITIONAL VALUES** (per portion): Energy 186.97 cal, Protein 1.27 gm, Carbohydrate 8.27 gm, Fat 16.42 gm

# GOBHI SAMOSA

*These triangular pockets of pastry filled with a spicy vegetable or curried minced meat are a popular Indian snack. They can be made substantial enough to constitute a light meal or dainty enough to serve as a cocktail savoury.*

## INGREDIENTS

### DOUGH

- ¾ cup plain flour *(maida)*
- ¼ cup fine semolina *(suji)*
- ¼ tsp salt
- a pinch of baking powder
- 30 g/1 oz (2 tbsp) ghee or butter or vegetable shortening

### VEGETABLE FILLING

- 3 tbsp oil
- 1 medium cauliflower - grated (2 cups)
- 1 boiled potato - mashed coarsely (½ cup)
- ½ inch/1 cm piece fresh ginger - grated
- ½ tsp red chilli powder
- salt to taste
- 1 tsp roasted, ground cumin seeds *(jeera)*
- ¼ tsp dry mango powder *(amchoor)*
- 1 tbsp each raisins & cashews - chopped
- 2 green chillies - deseeded and finely chopped
- ¼ tsp sugar

## METHOD

1. Sift flour, semolina, salt and baking powder into a bowl. Rub in ghee/butter/vegetable shortening. Add a few tablespoons of cold water to form a firm dough. Knead for 5-7 minutes until the dough becomes smooth and elastic. Cover the dough and keep aside for 30 minutes or longer while making the filling.

2. To prepare the filling, heat 3 tbsp oil in a pan. Remove from heat. Add ginger, salt, red chilli powder, ground cumin seeds and dry mango powder.

3. Return to heat. Add cashews. Cook for a few seconds. Add potatoes. Stir for a few seconds. Add cauliflower. Mix well. Add sugar and green chillies.

4. Cover and cook on low heat till the cauliflower is cooked. Make the filling spicy if you like. Keep aside.

5. Make lemon sized balls of the dough. Roll out into thin rounds. Cut each circle in half. Brush some water on the straight edges. Pick up the half circle and form a cone shape, overlapping straight edges 6 mm/¼ inch and pressing firmly to seal the seam. Fill cone two-thirds with the filling, about 1 tbsp of the filling in each cone. Press together to make a secure joint.

6. Deep fry in medium hot oil till golden. Let them be on low medium heat for 8-10 minutes to get cooked properly. Drain on absorbent paper towels and serve warm with mint or tamarind chutney.

Step 5

Step 5

**TIP:**
*Never fry the samosas on high heat and fry 8-10 pieces together in a single batch. If the oil is too hot, the outer covering gets browned very fast, without getting cooked properly.*

**NUTRITIONAL VALUES** (per portion): Energy 210.26 cal, Protein 2.69 gm, Carbohydrate 10.82 gm, Fat 17.35 gm

# MINT LASSI

Serves 4

*This yogurt smoothie is a very popular drink in the Northern part of India, specially Punjab. There are sweet and salty versions of this Indian drink. The savoury one given here is seasoned with roasted cumin and mint whereas the delicious sweet cooler is generally flavoured with rose water and cardamoms.*

## INGREDIENTS
- 4 tbsp finely chopped mint leaves (*pudina*)
- 1½ cups plain yogurt
- ½ tsp rock salt (*kala namak*)
- ½ tsp roasted, ground cumin seeds (*jeera*)
- ½ tsp salt, or to taste
- 3 cups water
- 6-8 ice cubes

## METHOD
1. Wash and finely chop mint leaves. Put yogurt, mint, cumin seeds, rock salt and salt in a blender. Blend for a few seconds.
2. Add chilled water and ice cubes. Blend till frothy.
3. Serve sprinkled with a pinch of ground, roasted cumin seeds and garnished with finely chopped mint.

**NUTRITIONAL VALUES** (per portion): Energy 45.00 cal, Protein 2.33 gm, Carbohydrate 2.25 gm, Fat 3.00 gm

# PUDINA JEERA PANI

Serves 4

*This is predominantly a summer drink which aids digestion. A savoury tamarind and mint cooler which is flavoured with roasted cumin seeds and black salt. This tangy cooler can be made as peppery as you like.*

## INGREDIENTS
- 4 cups water
- 4 tbsp seedless tamarind (*Imli*) or pulp
- 4 tsp fresh lime juice
- 3 tbsp sugar
- 1 inch/2.5 cm ginger - crushed roughly
- ¼ cup fresh mint leaves (*pudina*) - minced
- 1½ tsp ground roasted cumin (*bhuna jeera*)
- ½ tsp black salt (*kala namak*)
- salt to taste
- ½ tsp red chilli powder, or to taste, optional

## METHOD
1. Soak seedless tamarind in 1 cup hot water for 1 hour. Mash well. Add the remaining 3 cups water. Mash once again and strain to get tamarind water. If you are using tamarind pulp, add 4 cups of water to the pulp. If the pulp is salted, no salt is required in the jeera pani.
2. To the tamarind water, add all other ingredients — lime juice, crushed ginger, mint, black salt, ground roasted cumin, red chilli powder, sugar and salt to taste.
3. Mix well. Keep for 2 hours in the fridge to chill and for the flavours to penetrate.
4. At serving time, strain through a fine sieve. Adjust seasonings. Serve garnished with a lemon slice and mint.

**NUTRITIONAL VALUES** (per portion): Energy 39.49 cal, protein 0.02 gm, carbohydrate 9.80 gm, fat 0.02 gm

# GULNAR SEEKH KEBAB

*Succulent vegetarian kababs prepared from lentils. The colourful peppers on the outer surface give it an exotic look.*

## INGREDIENTS

- 1 cup split red lentils (*dhuli masoor ki dal*)
- 1 inch/2.5 cm piece ginger
- 8-10 flakes garlic
- 1 tsp cumin seeds (*jeera*)
- 1 tsp garam masala
- 1 tsp red chilli powder
- 3 slices bread - dipped in water & squeezed well
- 1 tsp salt, or to taste
- 3 tbsp oil
- 2 tbsp each of finely chopped green pepper, onion and red pepper

## TO SERVE

- 2 onions - cut into rings
- juice of 1 lemon
- a few mint leaves (*pudina*) - finely chopped

## METHOD

1. Soak lentils for 2 hours. Strain. Grind lentils, ginger, garlic and cumin seeds to a thick paste using the minimum amount of water. Keep the ground lentil paste aside.

2. Heat 3 tbsp oil in a heavy bottomed wok or a non stick pan. Add the lentil paste. Stir-fry for 4-5 minutes on low heat till lentils turn dry and stop sticking to the bottom of the pan. Remove from heat.

3. Remove sides of bread and dip in water for a second. Squeeze well and crumble finely. Mix bread, salt, garam masala and red chilli powder with the lentils. Mix well. Keep aside.

4. Heat oil in a pan for frying the kababs. Grease a wooden or a metal skewer. Spread a ball of lentil paste along the length of the skewer, such that it is inserted in the roll. Make a finger thick, 2 inch/5 cm long kebab of the lentil paste on the skewer.

5. Stick finely chopped onion and peppers on the kebab on the skewer, by pressing them on to the kebab.

6. Gently pull out the skewer and fry the seekh in medium hot oil till golden brown. Serve hot on a bed of onion rings sprinkled with lemon juice and chopped mint leaves.

Step 2

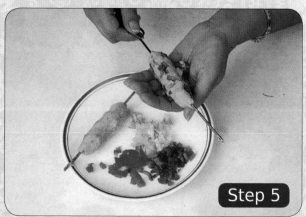

Step 5

**NUTRITIONAL VALUES** (per portion): Energy 155.38 cal, Protein 2.39 gm, Carbohydrate 6.80 gm, Fat 13.18 gm

# PANEER TIKKA

*Soft pieces of paneer cheese smeared with a flavoured yogurt paste and put in a tandoor or grilled in an oven to get a crisp and succulent snack.*

## INGREDIENTS

- 400 g/12 oz paneer (see page 28) - cut into 1 inch/2.5 cm cubes
- 1 green bell pepper - cut into 1" pieces
- 1 onion - cut into 1" pieces
- 1 tomato or ½ red bell pepper - seeded, cut into 1" pieces
- 1 tbsp chopped ginger
- 6-8 flakes garlic
- 1-2 dried, whole red chillies
- ¼ cup drained thick yogurt - (hang ½ cup yogurt for 30 minutes)
- 2 tbsp thick cream
- 1 tbsp gramflour
- 2 tbsp oil, preferably mustard oil
- a few drops of orange colour or a pinch of turmeric
- 1 tsp lemon juice
- ½ tsp rock salt *(kala namak)*
- 1 tsp tandoori masala (page 29)
- 1 tsp salt, or to taste
- ½ tsp ground cumin seeds *(jeera powder)*

## METHOD

1. Heat mustard oil in a pan. Add gramflour and stir fry on low flame till it gives a roasted aroma. Do not brown it.
2. Grind ginger, garlic and red chillies to a paste.
3. To the paste, add hung yogurt, cream, cornflour, ground cumin, lemon juice, salt, rock salt, tandoori masala and colour or ground turmeric. Add roasted gramflour along with the oil.
4. Marinate paneer, capsicum and onion pieces in it for at least 2 hours.
5. At the time of serving, grill paneer pieces and vegetables by placing them on a grill rack brushed with some oil.
6. After 5-7 minutes, baste paneer with some oil and change sides in between.
7. Grill the paneer till it starts getting crisp from the sides. Remove the vegetables and the paneer from the oven.
8. Serve hot with mint chutney.

**TIP:**
*A little kasoori methi crushed between the palms can be added to the marinade.*

**NUTRITIONAL VALUES** (per portion): Energy 275 cal, Protein 12.2 gm, Carbohydrate 2.6 gm, Fat 23.3 gm

# CHICKEN MALAI TIKKA

*Serves 4*

*Boneless pieces of chicken are barbecued till they turn crisp on the outside and soft from inside. Chicken is marinated with cream, cheese and eggs to keep the tikkas succulent. The tikkas are flavoured with ginger and garlic pastes.*

## INGREDIENTS

- 500 g/1 lb boneless chicken - cut into 2 inch/5 cm pieces
- 1 capsicum & 1 onion - cut into 1 inch/2.5 cm pieces
- 1 tomato - cut into 8 pieces and deseeded
- chaat masala or lemon juice to sprinkle

### FIRST MARINADE

- 2 tbsp vinegar
- 2 tbsp ginger-garlic paste
- ½ tsp salt or to taste
- ½ tsp red chilli powder

### SECOND MARINADE

- ½ cup thick drained yogurt (hang 1 cup for 30 minutes)
- ¼ cup thick cream
- 30 g/1 oz cheddar cheese - finely grated
- 1 egg
- 1 tbsp cornflour
- 1 tbsp finely chopped green chillies, optional
- 2 tbsp finely chopped coriander leaves
- ½ tsp salt
- ¼ tsp garam masala

## METHOD

1. Wash and pat dry the chicken pieces. Marinate the chicken pieces with the first marinade — salt, vinegar and ginger-garlic paste for 30 minutes.
2. Mix drained yogurt, cream, cheese, egg, cornflour, green chillies and coriander in a bowl. Add salt and garam masala. Marinate the chicken pieces in this mixture for 2-3 hours.
3. At serving time, mix capsicum, onion and tomato to the chicken in the marinade.
4. Arrange the chicken pieces on greased skewers, with the vegetables in between the chicken pieces. Heat a gas tandoor or an oven. Place the skewers on a grill or a wire rack, brushed with some oil. Grill for 15 minutes turning once in between. Cook till chicken turns tender.
5. Serve hot sprinkled with some lemon juice or chaat masala (page 29).

Step 2

**TIP:**
*To cook tikkas in the oven, place a drip tray under the wire rack on which the tikkas are placed, to collect the drippings.*

**NUTRITIONAL VALUES** (per portion): Energy 226.85 cal, Protein 38.28 gm, Carbohydrate 1.22 gm, Fat 7.58 gm

# POHA

Serves 4

*Flattened rice (also called beaten rice) is used to prepare this easily digestible snack. It makes a wonderful breakfast or teatime snack.*

### INGREDIENTS

- 2 cups flattened rice (*poha*)
- 1 medium onion - thinly sliced
- 1 tomato - finely chopped
- ½ cup green peas - boiled
- 6-8 green chillies - split
- a few curry leaves
- 1 tsp turmeric (*haldi*) powder
- 1 tsp mustard seeds (*rai*)
- pinch of asafoetida (*hing*)
- 1 tsp sugar, 1 tsp salt
- ½ cup chopped green coriander
- 2 tbsp lemon juice
- 2 tbsp oil

### METHOD

1. Put the poha in a strainer and wash under running water to moisten it lightly.
2. Heat oil. Add asafoetida and mustard seeds. When they stop crackling, add curry leaves and green chilies. Stir.
3. Add onions and stir till golden.
4. Add salt and turmeric powder. Stir.
5. Add chopped tomatoes and boiled peas and stir for a few minutes.
6. Flake the moistened poha with a fork and add it to the above masala. Mix well for 2-3 minutes.
7. Add lemon juice and coriander leaves and mix well. Serve.

**NUTRITIONAL VALUES** (per portion): Energy 221 cal, Protein 4 gm, Carbohydrate 30.06 gm, Fat 11.08 gm

# INSTANT IDLI

Serves 4

*Roasted semolina (suji) ground with curd is used to make this batter. Baking soda is used but no fermentation is required.*

### INGREDIENTS

- 1 cup semolina (*suji*)
- 1½ tbsp oil
- 1 cup yogurt (*dahi*)
- a few curry leaves
- ½ tsp baking soda (*mitha soda*)
- ¾ tsp salt
- ½ cup water, approx.

### METHOD

1. Heat 1½ tbsp oil in a kadhai. Add semolina and mix well. Stir on low heat for 2 minutes till it just starts to change colour. Remove from fire. Add salt. Mix well. Let it cool.
2. Add yogurt to the semolina (semolina should cool down). Mix well with a spoon or a wire whisk. Add baking soda. Mix very well till smooth. Keep the batter aside for 10 minutes. Take an idli mould and put 1-2 drops of oil in each round cup and spread it evenly with your fingers. Put 2-3 tbsp batter in each cup.
3. Put a big deep pan filled with 1" high water on fire, to boil. After the water boils, reduce heat. Place the idli mould into the pan of water. Increase heat to medium. Cover the pan with a lid. Steam for 14 minutes undisturbed on medium flame. Insert a knife in the idli, if it comes out clean it's done. Remove from fire. Remove idlis from the mould after 5 minutes with the help of a knife.
4. Serve hot with coconut chutney given on page 148 and sambhar given on page 100.

**NUTRITIONAL VALUES** (per portion): Energy 167 cal, Protein 4 gm, Carbohydrate 20.2 gm, Fat 7.7 gm

# FISH CAKES

*These wonderful fish cakes are a delight as an appetizer. A few green beans add to the taste and texture.*

## INGREDIENTS

- 300 g/10 oz fish - cut into small pieces, boneless and skinless
- 1 egg
- 2-3 big flakes of garlic - chopped roughly
- 6 tbsp cornflour
- 1 tsp salt, or to taste
- ½ tsp sugar
- ½ tsp red chilli powder, or to taste
- ½ tsp ground black pepper
- 2-3 tbsp chopped coriander leaves
- 60 g/2 oz green beans - chopped very finely
- egg white and bread crumbs to coat

## METHOD

1. Put fish, egg and garlic in a grinder & churn well to get a smooth mixture. Transfer to a bowl.

2. Mix all other ingredients including cornflour and beans. Mix well and check seasonings.

3. Shape into small patties. Beat egg white lightly with 1 tbsp water. Dip the patties in egg white and then press over bread crumbs to coat.

4. Deep fry till golden brown. Serve hot with any sauce or dip of your choice.

Step 2

**TIP:**
*Canned tuna makes wonderful fish cakes. Simply drain tuna and proceed the same way. Remember to check salt before adding as tuna is very salty.*

**NUTRITIONAL VALUES** (per portion): Energy 164.86 cal, Protein 6.48 gm, Carbohydrate 7.99 gm, Fat 11.89 gm

# PALAK PAKORAS

*Serves 6*

*Pakoras — deep-fried vegetable fritters made with a gram flour batter - have many variations. In this recipe, batter-coated spinach leaves make a crisp and delicious snack to serve at any time of the day.*

## INGREDIENTS

- 24 spinach (*palak*) leaves with 2" long stems

### BATTER

- ½ cup gram flour (*besan*)
- ¼ cup semolina (*suji*)
- ½ tsp carom seeds (*ajwain*)
- ½ tsp salt
- ¼ tsp red chilli powder
- ½ tsp coriander (*dhaniya*) powder
- ¾ cup water or as required
- oil to deep fry

## METHOD

1. Take spinach leaves including a little stem of about 2". Wash the spinach and pat dry on a clean kitchen towel.

2. Put all the ingredients for the batter in a bowl, adding enough water to make a thick batter with a coating consistency. Do not make it thin as it will not coat the leaves properly.

3. Heat the oil in a wok or kadhai.

4. Dip each spinach leaf in batter so that it gets well coated.

5. Fry the leaves on medium heat, a few at a time, till golden and crisp on both sides. Remove and drain on absorbent paper towels. Serve immediately.

**NUTRITIONAL VALUES** (per portion): Energy 145 cal, Protein 2 gm, Carbohydrate 5 gm, Fat 13 gm

# EGG PAKORAS

*Serves 4*

*Hard boiled eggs are dipped in a gram flour batter and deep fried. To serve, they are cut into halves to expose the yellow and white parts. Serve them as cocktail snacks.*

## INGREDIENTS

- 4 eggs - hard boiled
- salt & pepper to taste
- chaat masala to sprinkle (see page 29)

### BATTER

- ½ cup gram flour (*besan*)
- ¼ cup water (*approx.*)
- salt & pepper to taste
- ¼ tsp red chilli powder or paprika
- 2 tbsp chopped coriander

## METHOD

1. Boil eggs in water for 8 minutes or a little more till they become hard boiled. Peel. Sprinkle salt and pepper. Keep aside.

2. Mix all the ingredients of the batter together, adding just enough water to get a batter of medium pouring consistency, which is thick enough to coat the eggs. The batter should not be too thick as a thick coating does not taste good.

3. Dip eggs in batter and deep fry in oil on medium heat to golden brown. Remove on absorbent paper.

4. Cut the eggs vertically or horizontally into two or four pieces. Sprinkle chaat masala all over. Serve hot with tomato ketchup.

**NUTRITIONAL VALUES** (per portion): Energy 222.63 cal, Protein 16.95 gm, Carbohydrate 6.66 gm, Fat 14.23 gm

# SEEKH KEBAB

*Serves 8*

*These are long, finger shaped kababs of lamb mince. These may be served whole or cut into bite sized pieces.*

## INGREDIENTS

- 500 g/1 lb lamb mince *(keema)*
- 2 onions - sliced, deep fried to a crisp, brown colour and crushed
- 1 tsp garlic paste
  1 tsp ginger paste
- 2 tbsp cashews - soaked for 15 minutes in a little warm water & ground to a fine paste
- ¾ tsp garam masala powder
- salt to taste
- 1 tbsp raw papaya paste
- 2 tsp thick cream
- *chaat masala* to sprinkle (see page 29)

## METHOD

1. Wash the mince. Put in a strainer and gently press to squeeze out all the water.

2. Mix all the ingredients to the mince and knead well. Keep aside for 1 hour. Heat a gas oven or an electric oven with the skewers.

3. Take a big ball of the mince mixture and hold a hot skewer carefully in the other hand. Press the mince on to a hot skewer. The mince well immediately stick to the hot skewer. If the skewers are cold, the mince does not stick properly.

4. Repeat with left over mince on all the other skewers. Place the skewers in the oven. Keep rotating the skewers occasionally. When cooked, gently remove the kababs from the skewers with the help of a napkin.

5. Shallow fry the seekh kababs in a nonstick pan in 1 tbsp oil. To serve, sprinkle some chaat masala and lemon juice on the hot kababs.

**NUTRITIONAL VALUES** (per portion): Energy 95.65 cal, Protein 14.20 gm, Carbohydrate 2.55 gm, Fat 3.19 gm

# SHAMI KEBABS

*Serves 8*

*Discs of lamb mince mixed with some yellow split peas.*

## INGREDIENTS

### COOK TOGETHER

- 500 g/1 lb mutton mince *(keema)*
- ¼ cup split gram lentils *(channe ki dal)* - soaked for 15 minutes in water & drained
- 1 onion - sliced (½ cup)
- 1 tbsp chopped garlic
- 1 inch/2.5 cm piece ginger - chopped
- 2 tsp coriander seeds *(saboot dhaniya)*
- 1 tsp cumin seeds *(jeera)*
- 3-4 cloves *(laung)*
- 2 green cardamoms *(chhoti elaichi)*
- 2 brown cardamoms *(moti elaichi)*
- ½ inch/1 cm stick cinnamon *(dalchini)*
- 1 bay leaf *(tej patta)*
- 4-5 peppercorns *(saboot kali mirch)*
- 2-3 dry, whole red chillies
- salt to taste, ½ cup water

## METHOD

1. Wash the mince and drain out the water well through a strainer. Press well to squeeze out all the water.

2. Add all the ingredients to the mince and cook in a heavy bottomed pan on medium heat till done or pressure cook to give 2 whistles. Keep on low heat for 2 minutes after the whistles. Remove from heat.

3. When the pressure drops, uncover the pressure cooker. If there is any water left, keep the cooker on heat to dry the water. If the mince is wet, the kebabs break while frying, so dry it well.

4. Dry grind the dried minced meat either on stone grinder or in a food processor till smooth without adding any water while grinding.

5. To prepare the kebabs, make tiny balls. Flatten them into small discs. Shallow fry in oil in a non stick pan on medium heat, till brown on both sides.

**NUTRITIONAL VALUES** (per portion): Energy 113.35 cal, Protein 14.54 gm, Carbohydrate 3.95 gm, Fat 4.40 gm

# AJWAINI MURG

*A generous quantity of carom seeds with some crushed red chillies are used to spice up this quick preparation of chicken.*

## INGREDIENTS

- 1 chicken (750 g/1½ lb) - cut into 6-8 pieces, or 8 drumsticks
- ½ cup yogurt (*dahi*)
- 2 tsp carom seeds (*ajwain*)
- 1 tbsp ginger-garlic paste
- 1 tsp red chilli flakes or red chilli paste
- 1 tsp salt or to taste
- 3 tbsp oil
- ½ cup thick cream
- ½ cup fresh green coriander - chopped

## METHOD

1. Marinate the chicken with yogurt, carom seeds, ginger-garlic paste, red chilli and salt for 30 minutes.

2. Heat oil in a heavy bottomed pan. Add the chicken pieces leaving behind the marinade.

3. Cook on high heat till the chicken turns brown and all the juices get absorbed. Do not overlap the pieces of chicken while browning.

4. Lower the heat. Add the marinade which is left behind. Mix well for a minute.

5. Add ½ cup of water. Cover and cook on low heat, till the chicken turns tender.

6. Add cream and coriander. Stir fry till the chicken is dry and coated with coriander. Serve hot.

Step 1

**TIP:**
*A little dry fenugreek (kasoori methi) can be added to the marinade for a different flavour.*

**NUTRITIONAL VALUES** (per portion): Energy 170.00 cal, Protein 22.10 gm, Carbohydrate 0.50 gm, Fat 8.83 gm

# VEGETARIAN CURRIES

Indian vegetarian curries are aromatic, magically spiced wet gravies. These when thin are devoured with some rice and if a curry calls for a thick gravy, it is generally relished more with flat breads. The procedure for making curries is simple, but each ingredient should be added in it's correct sequence of cooking and stir fried on low heat to impart all of it's flavour to the curry. Whole masalas added to hot oil in the beginning, add a lot of flavour to the curry.

Curries may be brownish in colour because the onions are cooked till brown. This imparts colour to the curry. Tomato based curries are reddish in colour. Some time yogurt based curries are whitish in colour. Curries have a hint of yellow because of the ground turmeric added to them.

# MIRCHON KI SABZI

*A delicious curry made without onion and garlic. Add few boiled corn kernels can also be added along with the potatoes for the filling.*

## INGREDIENTS

- 9-10 thick green chilies or jalapenos (*achaari mirch*)
- 4-5 potatoes – boiled and mashed (2 cups)
- 1½ tsp finely chopped ginger
- ½ tsp salt or to taste
- 1½ tsp chaat masala
- ½ red chilli powder
- ¼ tsp garam masala
- 2 tbsp yogurt (*dahi*)
- 1 tsp lemon juice
- a pinch of black salt (*kala namak*)
- 2 tbsp butter

### GRAVY

- 4 tomatoes – boil in water for 3-4 minutes, peel and grind to a fine paste
- 3 tbsp oil
- 1 tsp cumin seeds (*jeera*)
- ½ tsp salt or to taste
- 3 tbsp cream
- ¼ tsp red chili powder
- ¼ tsp turmeric (*haldi*) powder
- ¼ tsp garam masala
- 1½ cups water

## METHOD

1. Slit and deseed green chillies. Boil water in a pan. Put green chillies in boiling water and remove from fire. Take out green chillies from hot water after a minute.

2. In a pan heat 2 tbsp butter. Add finely chopped ginger and stir till golden. Add potatoes, salt, chaat masala, red chili powder, garam masala, yogurt, lemon juice and black salt. Sauté on low heat for 5 minutes to prepare a nice masala. Remove from fire and cool.

3. Fill each green chilli with this masala nicely.

4. For the gravy, heat oil in a pan, add cumin seeds. When they splutter add pureed tomatoes, salt, garam masala, chaat masala, turmeric powder and red chili powder. Saute for 7-8 minutes till oil separates.

5. Add cream. Saute for 2-3 minutes. If there is any filling remaining, add filling in the gravy masala and mix well for 2 minutes.

6. Add the stuffed green chillies and put 1 cup water to get a thick gravy. Cover and cook on low heat for 5-7 minutes.

7. When the green chilies are cooked remove from fire and serve hot with chappatis.

**TIP:**
*Enjoy mirchi ke pakore by dipping the stuffed chillies in gramflour batter and deep frying in hot oil. You can prepare the batter as given for palak ke pakore on page 52*

**NUTRITIONAL VALUES** (per portion): Energy 178 cal, Protein 1.6 gm, Carbohydrate 20 gm, Fat 10.2 gm

# PALAK ALOO

*Spinach and potatoes flavoured with cloves — an excellent blend to make the dish superb. Boiled potatoes may be substituted for raw ones, if you want to prepare the vegetable in a jiffy.*

## INGREDIENTS

- 500 g/1 lb spinach (*paalak*)
- 2 small potatoes
- 1 inch/2.5 cm piece ginger - grated
- 3 tbsp oil or ghee
- 2 black cardamoms (*moti elaichi*)
- 1 inch/2.5 cm stick cinnamon (*dalchini*)
- 5-6 flakes garlic - crushed to a rough paste
- 2 onions - finely chopped (1 cup)
- 3 tomatoes - chopped (1½ cups)
- ½ tsp turmeric powder (*haldi*)
- 1 tsp ground coriander (*dhaniya powder*)
- ½ tsp red chilli powder
- ½ tsp garam masala
- 1 tsp salt, or to taste

## METHOD

1. Wash and peel potatoes. Cut into 1 inch/2.5 cm pieces. Cut away thick stalks of spinach. Chop leaves finely into thin strips or ribbons.

2. Heat oil. Reduce heat. Add black cardamoms and cinnamon. Wait for a minute. Add garlic and cook till it starts to change colour.

3. Add onions and stir fry till golden. Reduce heat. Add turmeric powder, ground coriander, chilli powder, garam masala and salt. Mix well on low heat for a minute.

4. Add ginger. Stir for a few seconds. Add tomatoes and stir fry for 3-4 minutes till well blended.

5. Add potatoes. Stir fry for 4-5 minutes. Cook covered for 10 minutes, sprinkling a little water occasionally, till the potatoes turn soft.

6. Add spinach. Continue cooking, without covering, for about 10 minutes, till the spinach gets wilted and is well blended with the potatoes.

7. Serve hot with any bread.

Step 5

Step 6

**NUTRITIONAL VALUES** (per portion): Energy 105.42 cal, Protein 2.34 gm, Carbohydrate 5.67 gm, Fat 8.13 gm

# PANEER MAKHANI

*Serves 6*

*Paneer cheese is added to a fragrant tomato curry cooked in butter. You may substitute paneer with potatoes and peas if you like and turn it into makhani aloo matar.*

## INGREDIENTS

- 250 g/8 oz paneer - cut into 1 inch/2.5 cm pieces

### GRAVY

- 3 tbsp butter or oil
- 2 onions - chopped (1 cup)
- 1 green chilli - deseeded and chopped
- 1 tsp chopped ginger
- ¼ tsp red chilli powder
- 6-7 tomatoes (500 g/1 lb) - chopped
- ¼ cup yogurt (*dahi*) - whisked till smooth
- 3 tbsp cashews - soaked in a little water for 15 minutes & ground to a paste
- 1½ tsp salt, or to taste
- ¾ tsp garam masala
- ½-1 tsp sugar, or to taste
- ½ cup thin fresh cream or milk
- 1 tbsp tomato ketchup

## METHOD

1. Heat 2 tbsp butter or oil in a pan. Add onions, green chilli and ginger. Cook on low heat until onions turn transparent. Add red chilli powder. Stir. Add chopped tomatoes. Cover and cook for 7-8 minutes till the tomatoes turn pulpy.

2. Add yogurt. Cook till the mixture turns dry and reddish again.

3. Remove from heat. Cool. Grind to a very smooth puree with ½ cup water. Heat 1 tbsp of butter or oil in a wok or a kadhai. Add the prepared tomato-yogurt puree. Stir fry for 3-4 minutes on low heat.

4. Add salt, garam masala, sugar and tomato ketchup. Mix. Add cashew paste. Cook on low heat for 1-2 minutes.

5. Add enough milk or very thin fresh cream, to get a thick pouring consistency of the gravy. Add paneer pieces. Give one boil on low heat. Remove from heat. Transfer to a serving dish.

6. Garnish with a swirl of cream, a few coriander leaves and ginger matchsticks. Serve with naans, paranthas or any other bread.

Step 1

Step 2

**TIP:**
*Paneer may be prepared as given on page 28. You may get something very similar to paneer by baking ricotta cheese in the oven at 350°F for about 30 minutes. Cut the baked ricotta into cubes after it cools down a little.*

**NUTRITIONAL VALUES** (per portion): Energy 323.42 cal, Protein 15.74 gm, Carbohydrate 13.59 gm, Fat 22.82 gm

# SHAHI KAAJU ALOO

*Serves 8-10*

*Potatoes are simmered in a delicious, pale yellow gravy. Curd and cashews form the base of this royal (shahi) curry. Black cumin lends it's royal flavour to the humble potatoes.*

## INGREDIENTS

- 300 g/10 oz (4) potatoes
- 4 tbsp cashews - soaked in ¼ cup water
- 1 tbsp chopped ginger
- 1 tsp chopped garlic
- ½ tsp black cumin (*shah jeera*)
- 1 bay leaf (*tej patta*)
- 2 onions - chopped (1 cup)
- a pinch of turmeric (*haldi*)
- ¼ tsp garam masala
- 2 tbsp chopped coriander
- ¼ cup yogurt (*dahi*) - whisked to make it smooth
- ¼ cup milk
- oil for frying and 4 tbsp oil

## METHOD

1. Wash potatoes and peel. Cut potatoes into 1 inch/2.5 cm pieces.

2. Fry the potatoes to a deep golden brown and keep aside.

3. Grind cashews, ginger and garlic to a paste in a small coffee or spice grinder. Keep cashew paste aside.

4. Heat 4 tbsp oil in a heavy bottomed pan. Add black cumin and bay leaf. Wait for 30 seconds till cumin stops spluttering. Add onions and cook on low heat till onions turn soft but do not let them turn brown. Add turmeric and garam masala. Stir to mix well.

5. Add cashew paste. Cook for 1 minute. Add yogurt and stir fry till water evaporates. Cook till dry.

6. Add milk and about ½ cup water to get a gravy. Boil and simmer for 2-3 minutes.

7. Add the fried potatoes and chopped coriander to the gravy. Cook on low heat till the gravy gets thick and coats the potatoes. Serve hot with rotis or paranthas.

Step 1

Step 3

**NUTRITIONAL VALUES** (per portion): Energy 119.10 cal, Protein 1.93 gm, Carbohydrate 8.48 gm, Fat 8.59 gm

# BAGHAARE BAINGAN

*A famous Hyderabadi brinjal curry. Roasted onions are combined with mild spices & stuffed in small brinjals. Tamarind & jaggery give this curry a sweet and sour taste.*

## INGREDIENTS

- 300 gm/10 oz brinjals (small round variety)
- 2 onions - cut each into 4-6 pieces
- 2 tsp roughly chopped ginger
- 1 tbsp chopped garlic
- 1 tsp coriander seeds (*saboot dhaniya*)
- 1½ tbsp sesame seeds (*til*)
- 3 tbsp roasted peanuts
- ½ tsp cumin seeds (*jeera*)
- 1 tsp poppy seeds (*khus khus*)
- 1 inch square piece dry coconut (*kopra*)
- a pinch fenugreek seeds (*methi dana*)
- ¼ tsp turmeric powder (*haldi*)
- ½ tsp red chilli powder
- ½ tsp jaggery (*gur*) or sugar
- a small marble size ball tamarind - soak in 1 cup hot water for 15 minutes, mash and strain
- a few curry leaves
- 6 tbsp oil
- ½ tsp salt or to taste

## METHOD

1. Wash brinjals. Make cross-slits along the length of the brinjal ensuring that the brinjal is held together at the stem. Keep aside.

2. Roast the onions in a pan for 8-10 minutes, till they soften a little and turn slightly golden brown. Remove from pan.

3. Then dry roast together, for a minute over medium heat, the coriander seeds, sesame seeds, peanuts, cumin seeds, poppy seeds, dry coconut and fenugreek seeds till they darken slightly and give out a roasted smell.

4. Grind together the onions, roasted spices, ginger, garlic, salt, turmeric, red chilli powder and jaggery/sugar to a fine paste. Using only about 4-5 tbsp of this paste, stuff the brinjals. Keep stuffed brinjals aside. Add tamarind water to the remaining paste.

5. Heat oil in a pan, add curry leaves and after a few seconds, add the stuffed brinjals. Shake the pan instead of stirring, to brown the brinjals evenly, for about 10 minutes.

6. Add the ground spice paste mixed with tamarind water. Cook covered over medium heat for 5-7 minutes. Add ½ cup water and stir occasionally till brinjals get tender and oil separates. Serve hot.

**TIP:**
*Rub a pinch of salt inside each brinjal which is slit. Keep aside for 15 minutes for them to sweat. Rinse. This help to remove the little bitterness in the brinjals.*

**NUTRITIONAL VALUES** (per portion): Energy 204.5 cal, Protein 2.9 gm, Carbohydrate 6 gm, Fat 18.5 gm

*Serves 4*

*Potato dumplings (koftas) with colourful vegetable filling. The colours are exposed by dividing each kofta into two. Served on a bed of red, cardamom flavoured curry.*

## INGREDIENTS

### KOFTA COVERING

- 4 potatoes - boiled & grated (2 cups)
- 4 slices bread - dipped in water & squeezed
- ¾ tsp salt, or to taste
- ½ tsp black pepper
- pinch of baking powder
- 2 tsp tomato ketchup

### KOFTA FILLING

- 1 tbsp oil
- 1 carrot - grated thickly (½ cup)
- 1 capsicum - shredded (½ cup)
- 3-4 tbsp shredded green cabbage
- ¼ cup grated cheddar cheese
- salt, pepper to taste

### GRAVY

- 4 tbsp oil
- 2 black cardamoms *(moti elaichi)*
- 2 onions - chopped (1 cup)
- 3 tomatoes - chopped (1½ cups)
- 2 tsp finely grated ginger
- 1½ tsp ground coriander *(dhaniya powder)*
- ½ tsp each red chilli powder & garam masala
- ¾ cup milk
- 1 tbsp tomato ketchup
- salt to taste

## METHOD

1. For the kofta covering, in a bowl mix all the ingredients given under kofta covering till well blended. Divide into 4 big balls. Keep aside.

2. For the filling, heat 1 tbsp oil. Add vegetables and saute for 2 minutes. Sprinkle some salt and pepper to taste. Remove from fire. Add cheese.

3. Flatten each potato ball to a size of about 3 inch/8 cm diameter. Place 1 tbsp of filling in the centre. Lift the sides to cover the filling.

4. Give the kofta an oval shape like an egg. Deep fry koftas, one at a time, carefully to a golden brown colour.

5. To prepare the gravy, grind onions, tomatoes and half the ginger together. Heat oil. Add cardamoms and wait for 30-40 seconds. Add onion-tomato paste and cook on medium heat till well dried. Add ground coriander and red chilli powder. Stir fry till oil comes to the surface.

6. Reduce heat. Add milk gradually, 2-3 tbsp at a time, stirring continuously till all the milk is used. Cook on low heat till the mixture turns red again and the oil separates.

7. Add enough water to get a thin curry. Boil. Add salt, garam masala, tomato ketchup and cook on low heat for 8-10 minutes till it thickens slightly. Keep aside.

8. To serve, cut koftas into two. Boil the gravy separately, and pour in a serving dish. Arrange the koftas on the gravy and microwave for a couple of minutes to heat the koftas. Serve immediately with rice or bread.

Step 3

**NUTRITIONAL VALUES** (per portion): Energy 339.49 cal, Protein 9.14 gm, Carbohydrate 27.05 gm, Fat 21.54 gm

# TANDOORI & KADHAI – VEGETARIAN

The traditional Indian tandoor is a clay oven, which imparts a smoky flavour to the food. You may prepare these succulent tandoori dishes very conveniently in your electric oven. These dishes are crisp on the outside but soft and succulent from inside. Kadhai is the most commonly used utensil in Indian cooking. It is a deep frying pan, round bottomed with two handles on the sides, resembling a wok. These oven baked tandoori dishes and semi-dry kadhai dishes make excellent accompaniment to all your meals.

# TANDOORI VEGETABLES WITH BARBECUE SAUCE

*Serves 4*

*Assorted vegetables smeared with a ginger-garlic flavoured yogurt paste and barbecued in a grill or a tandoor, which is a clay oven. These are wonderful when served with a sauce.*

## INGREDIENTS
- 6-8 babycorns
- 1 green bell pepper
- 8 cherry tomatoes or 1 large tomato
- 200 g/6 oz (10-12) button mushrooms
- 250 g/8 oz paneer (see page 28)
- 1 onion

## MARINADE
- 1 cup thick yogurt (*dahi*) - hang for 30 minutes
- 2 tbsp thick cream
- 2 tbsp cornflour
- ½ tsp black salt
- ½ tsp garam masala
- ½ tsp red chilli powder
- ¾ tsp salt, or to taste

## BARBECUE SAUCE
- 4 tbsp oil
- 1 small onion - very finely chopped
- 1 tbsp finely chopped celery
- 8-10 flakes garlic - crushed (1 tbsp)
- 4 large tomatoes - blanched and puree
- ¼ cup tomato puree
- ½ tsp red chilli paste or paprika
- 2 tsp worcestershire sauce
- 2 tsp soya sauce
- ½ tsp pepper
- 1 tsp salt, or to taste
- ½ tsp sugar
- 1 cup water, approx.

## METHOD

1. Cut paneer and green peppers into large (1½ inch/4 cm) cubes. Leave cherry tomatoes whole but if the tomato is large, cut it into 8 pieces and remove the pulp. Trim the ends of the stalks of mushrooms, leaving them whole. Cut the onion into four and separate the leaves. Blanch baby corns in hot salted water for 2 minutes.

2. Mix all ingredients of the marinade in a large mixing bowl. Add paneer first and mix well. Add all the other vegetables and mix gently so as not to break the paneer pieces. Marinate for at least 30 minutes or till serving time.

3. At serving time, arrange paneer and vegetables on greased skewers. Grill skewers in an oven at 210°C/410°F for about 12 minutes or roast in a gas tandoor. If you do not posses skewers, place the marinated vegetables directly on the grill brushed with some oil.

4. For the barbecue sauce, heat oil in a wok or a deep pan. Add onion and celery, stir till onion turns light golden. Add garlic. Stir. Add tomatoes, tomato puree and chilli paste. Stir continuously and cook for 5 minutes till oil separates.

5. Add soya sauce, worcestershire sauce, salt and pepper. Add enough water to get a saucy consistency. Boil. Simmer for 5 minutes. Add sugar if needed.

6. To serve, spread the hot sauce in a platter. Keeping the vegetable skewers on the sauce, pull out the skewers carefully to get an arranged line of paneer and vegetables on the sauce. Remove vegetables in the same way from all skewers. Serve hot with rice if you like.

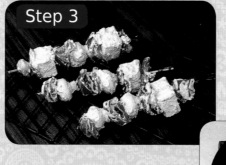

Step 3

Step 4

**NUTRITIONAL VALUES** (per portion): Energy 353 cal, Protein 11.7 gm, Carbohydrate 12.5 gm, Fat 18.95 gm

# KADHAI MUSHROOMS

*Serves 4*

*A semi dry preparation of fresh mushrooms flavoured with coriander and fenugreek.*

## INGREDIENTS

- 200 g/6 oz fresh button mushrooms
- 1 green pepper - cut into ½ inch/1 cm pieces
- 2 onions - finely chopped (1 cup)
- 1 inch/2.5 cm piece ginger
- 5-6 flakes garlic
- 3 tomatoes - chopped finely (1½ cups)
- 1-2 dry, whole red chillies, optional
- 1 tbsp coriander seeds (*saboot dhaniya*)
- ¼ tsp fenugreek seeds (*methi dana*)
- 1 tsp salt, or to taste
- 1 tbsp dry fenugreek leaves (*kasoori methi*) - crushed
- 2 green chillies - cut into thin long strips, optional
- 2 tbsp chopped coriander
- 4 tbsp oil

## METHOD

1. Grind ginger and garlic to a paste. Grind together, dry, whole red chillies and coriander seeds coarsely. Wash mushrooms well in plenty of water to remove any dirt. If mushrooms are small, keep them whole, if big, cut into halves. Wipe dry.

2. Heat 4 tbsp oil. Add mushrooms. Cook on medium heat, stirring occasionally, for 10 minutes till they turn brown and get cooked.

3. Remove mushrooms from oil.

4. In the same oil, add fenugreek seeds. When they turn golden, add chopped onions and stir till light brown.

5. Add ginger-garlic paste. Cook for ½ minute. Add coriander-chilli powder. Stir. Add chopped tomatoes. Cook for 7-8 minutes, till oil separates. Add dry fenugreek greens and salt.

6. Add green peppers. Stir well. Add ¼ cup water. Add the cooked mushrooms and chopped coriander. Stir-fry for 2-3 minutes. Remove from heat. Garnish with slit green chillies. Serve with any type of bread.

Step 2

Step 5

**NUTRITIONAL VALUES** (per portion): Energy 171.5 cal, Protein 1.6 gm, Carbohydrate 5.7 gm, Fat 15.3 gm

# TANDOORI ARBI

*Serves 6*

*Taro root or colocasia, makes an excellent side dish. Carom seeds aid the digestion of this vegetable, besides lending it's flavour to it.*

## INGREDIENTS

- 500 g/1 lb colocasia *(arbi)* - 2 inch/5 cm long
- 1 cup yogurt *(dahi)* - hang for 30 minutes
- 1 tbsp *tandoori or chaat masala* (see page 29)
- ½ tsp salt
- 1 tsp carom seeds *(ajwain)*
- 2 tsp ginger-garlic paste
- ½ tbsp cornflour
- 4 tbsp oil
- 2 onions - sliced (1 cup)
- 1 tsp ground coriander *(dhaniya powder)*
- ½ tsp garam masala
- ½ tsp dried mango powder *(amchoor)*
- ½ tbsp shredded ginger

## METHOD

1. Boil colocasia in salted water for 10-12 minutes till done. Remove from heat. Strain. Peel colocasia. Cut each into two pieces. Flatten each piece slightly.

2. Hang yogurt in a muslin cloth for about 30 minutes to let the liquid drain out. Mix 1 tbsp oil, ½ tsp salt and tandoori masala or chaat masala to yogurt. Add ginger-garlic paste, cornflour and ½ tsp crushed carom seeds also. Marinate the colocasia pieces in it for 15-20 minutes.

3. Brush the oven rack or an oven proof dish with some oil. Arrange the colocasia on the rack or in the dish. Keep in a moderately hot oven at 190°C/375°F for 20 minutes, till the yogurt dries up and forms a coating. Remove from the oven and keep aside.

4. Heat 3 tbsp oil in a non stick pan. Reduce heat. Add ½ tsp carom seeds. After a few seconds when they turn golden, add sliced onions. Cook till onions turn light brown. Add the ground coriander, garam masala, dry mango powder and ¼ tsp salt. Add the colocasia pieces.

5. Add the shredded ginger. Mix well. Stir fry for 3-4 minutes, adding a few teaspoons of oil, if it sticks to the pan. Remove from heat. Serve hot with onion rings and lemon wedges as a side dish.

Step 1

Step 2

**NUTRITIONAL VALUES** (per portion): Energy 201.83 cal, Protein 3.85 gm, Carbohydrate 20.98 gm, Fat 11.44 gm

# GREEN BEANS WITH SESAME SEEDS

*Serves 4*

*Green Beans with sesame seeds spark the look and flavour of this ordinary vegetable. Remember to cut the beans into slightly longer pieces, about 2 inch/5 cm, to make them look more appetizing.*

## INGREDIENTS

- 200 g/6 oz green beans - threaded and cut into 2 inch/5 cm long pieces
- 1 tomato - quartered
- 2 tbsp dried fenugreek leaves (*kasoori methi*)
- 2 tbsp oil
- 1 tsp sesame seeds (*til*) - dry roasted, to garnish

### SPICE MIXTURE (GRIND TOGETHER WITH A FEW TBSP OF WATER)

- 2 tsp white sesame seeds (*safed til*)
- 1 tsp cumin seeds (*jeera*)
- 1 tsp ground coriander (*dhaniya*)
- ½ tsp red chilli powder
- ¼ tsp turmeric (*haldi*)
- 1 tsp salt, or to taste
- 1 big onion - chopped roughly (¾ cup)
- 2 flakes garlic

## METHOD

1. To prepare the spice mixture, grind onion with cumin seeds, sesame seeds, coriander powder, red chilli powder, garlic and turmeric with a little water to a fine paste in a coffee or spice grinder.

2. Heat 2 tbsp oil in a pan or a wok. Reduce heat. Add the spice mixture and fry for about 2 minutes, stirring continuously.

3. Add tomato pieces, beans and fenugreek. Stir fry for 5 minutes.

4. Cover and cook for 10-15 minutes or till the beans turn soft. Do not overcook them. Serve sprinkled with a few roasted sesame seeds with any type of bread.

Step 2

Step 3

**NUTRITIONAL VALUES** (per portion): Energy 90.06 cal, Protein 1.18 gm, Carbohydrate 4.26 gm, Fat 7.57 gm

# MAKAI PALAK

*Babycorns and spinach flavoured with fragrant green cardamoms and cloves makes this side dish a delight. You may substitute sweet corn kernels for babycorns.*

## INGREDIENTS

- 500 g/1 lb spinach (*palak*)
- 100 g/4 oz babycorns - cut into half lengthwise
- 1 tbsp lemon juice
- 1 tsp sugar
- 1 tsp salt
- a pinch of turmeric (*haldi*)
- 3-4 tbsp oil
- ½ tsp cumin seeds (*jeera*)
- 1 tbsp finely chopped garlic
- 2 dry, red chillies - broken
- 1 large onion - cut into rings
- 1 tomato - finely chopped
- ¾ tsp salt or to taste
- 1 tsp coriander (*dhaniya*) powder
- ½ tsp garam masala

### CRUSH TOGETHER

- 1 clove (*laung*) and 1 green cardamom (*chhoti elaichi*)

## METHOD

1. Cut away thick stalks of spinach. Cut into thin strips or ribbon.

2. Wash the spinach nicely. Place in a strainer and squeeze out excess water.

3. Heat 3 cups water in a pan. Add lemon juice, sugar, 1 tsp salt and a pinch of turmeric. Bring to a boil and add babycorns. Boil for 1-2 minutes. Strain.

4. Heat oil in a wok or a large kadhai. Add cumin seeds. Let them turn golden. Add garlic, red chillies and onion rings. Stir for ½ minute till garlic changes colour.

5. Add the spinach and ¼ tsp salt. Stir fry till dry and well fried. Add garam masala and coriander powder. Add tomato and cook for a minute.

6. Add baby corns, cook for 5 minutes till tomatoes are slightly soft and the spinach blends with the baby corns.

7. Add the crushed spices and mix well. Serve.

Step 5

**TIP:**
*A little sugar added to greens while cooking helps to retain the green colour of the vegetable. Also, never cover the greens while cooking because they lose their vibrant colour when covered during cooking.*

**NUTRITIONAL VALUES** (per portion): Energy 208 cal, Protein 4.45 gm, Carbohydrate 11.6 gm, Fat 16 gm

# TANDOORI CAULIFLOWER

*Whole cauliflower is baked with a ginger-garlic flavoured yogurt masala stuffed within the florets. Onion rings and fresh coriander topping adds to the taste.*

## INGREDIENTS

- 3 small cauliflowers, each about 315 g/10 oz

### MARINADE

- 1½ cups thick yogurt - hang for 30 minutes to give about ¾ cup hung yogurt
- 2 tbsp ginger-garlic paste
- 2 tsp tandoori masala (see page 29)
- ¼ tsp salt, or to taste
- 2 pinches of turmeric for colour
- ½ tsp red chilli powder
- 2 tbsp oil

### TOPPING

- 2 tbsp oil
- 4-5 small onions - cut into fine rings (1 cup)
- ¼ cup tomato puree
- 3-4 tbsp chopped fresh coriander
- 1 green chilli - deseeded and chopped
- salt to taste
- 1 tsp *tandoori masala* (see page 29)

## METHOD

1. Boil 5-6 cups of water in a large pan with 2 tsp salt. Add the cauliflowers to the boiling water. Cook for 2-3 minutes till just tender. Do not cook for too long. Remove from water and dry well on a clean kitchen napkin. Keep aside.

2. Mix all ingredients of the marinade in a bowl. Apply the marinade on the cauliflower, inserting some marinade inside the florets. Turn the cauliflower and insert some marinade from the backside also. Marinate the cauliflowers for at least 1 hour.

3. Place the marinated cauliflowers on a grill rack and grill in a hot oven at 200°/400°F till crisp and golden. Remove and keep on the serving platter.

4. To prepare the topping, heat 2 tbsp oil in pan. Add onion rings. When they start turning brown, add tomato puree. Stir. Add fresh coriander, green chillies and tandoori masala. Adjust salt and seasonings.

5. To serve, spread some onion topping on the grilled cauliflowers. Heat in a microwave or an oven. Serve hot with rice or bread.

Step 2

Step 3

**NUTRITIONAL VALUES** (per portion): Energy 112.24 cal, Protein 3.29 gm, Carbohydrate 3.93 gm, Fat 9.26 gm

# PESHAWARI BROCCOLI

*Broccoli florets with long stalks are flavoured with roasted cashews, cardamom seeds and barbecued.*

## INGREDIENTS

- 500 g/1 lb (2 medium heads) broccoli - cut into medium sized florets with long stalks
- 2 tsp salt
- 1 tsp sugar

### 1ST MARINADE

- juice of 1 lemon (3-4 tsp)
- ¾ tsp carom seeds *(ajwain)*
- 1 tsp salt and ½ tsp red chilli powder

### 2ND MARINADE

- 1 cup thick yogurt - hang for 30 minutes or more
- 4 tbsp roasted or fried cashews - grind to a thick paste with little water
- ½ cup thick cream
- 2 tsp ginger paste
- ½ tsp red chilli paste, optional
- ½ tsp salt
- ½ tsp cumin powder
- ¼ tsp garam masala
- 2 tbsp oil
- 1 clove *(laung)* - crushed
- seeds of 1 green cardamom - crushed

## METHOD

1. Boil 5-6 cups of water in a large pan. Add 2 tsp salt and 1 tsp sugar to the water. Add broccoli pieces to the boiling water. Boil. Keep on boiling for 2 minutes. Drain. Wipe the pieces well with a clean kitchen towel till well dried.

2. Spread the broccoli on a flat plate and sprinkle the ingredients of the 1st marinade. Marinate the broccoli for 15 minutes.

3. Drain the broccoli of any excess liquid. Mix all the ingredients of the 2nd marinade. Add the broccoli to it and mix well. Check the salt and add more if needed. Keep in the refrigerator till the time of serving.

4. Brush the grill of the oven or gas tandoor with some oil. Place the broccoli spears on it and barbecue them in a gas oven for 10 minutes or grill in a preheated electric oven at 210°C/410°F only for 10 minutes. Do not over grill it, it turns too dry. Serve hot as a side dish.

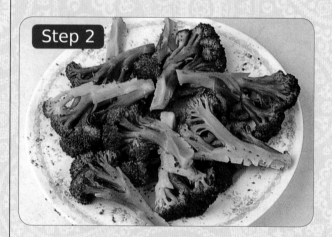

Step 2

Step 3

**NUTRITIONAL VALUES** (per portion): Energy 125.00 cal, Protein 8.93 gm, Carbohydrate 11.00 gm, Fat 4.88 gm

# ACHAARI ALOO

*A perfect combination of spices are popped into hot oil to impart all flavour. This tempering is then poured over a sweet and sour preparation of potatoes to enhance the taste and look of the humble potatoes.*

## INGREDIENTS

- 500 g/1 lb potatoes
- 4 medium onions
- 1 bay leaf (*tej patta*)
- 1½ tsp ginger paste
- 1½ tsp garlic paste
- 1½ tsp red chilli powder
- ½ tsp turmeric powder (*haldi*)
- 1 tsp salt or to taste
- oil for frying

### MIX TOGETHER

- ¼ cup vinegar
- 2 tsp sugar

### TEMPERING (BAGHAAR)

- 2 tbsp oil
- 1 tsp nigella seeds (*kalaunji*)
- ½ tsp mustard seeds (*rai*)
- 1 tsp cumin seeds (*jeera*)
- 8 dry whole red chillies

## METHOD

1. Boil and peel potatoes. Cut into 1 inch/2.5 cm pieces.
2. Peel and grind onions to a paste.
3. Heat oil for frying in a pan or kadhai. Fry potatoes till golden-brown in colour. Keep aside.
4. Heat 6 tbsp oil. Add bay leaf and onions and fry for 8-10 minutes on medium flame till golden brown.
5. Add ginger and garlic and fry for a minute. Add salt, turmeric, red chilli powder. Mix well. Add 2 tbsp water. Bring to a boil.
6. Add fried potatoes and mix well gently. Add about ½ cup water and cook on low heat for about 5 minutes till the spices are well-blended and a slight gravy, remains.
7. Remove from fire and add sugar and vinegar water. Mix well gently. Transfer to the serving dish.
8. Heat 2 tbsp oil, add the nigella seeds, mustard seeds and cumin seeds. Add whole red chillies. When the cumin seeds begin to turn golden and the red chillies darken, pour the tempering over the dish.

Step 3

Step 4

**TIP:**
*A special spice blend called panch phoran - meaning "five spices" can be used for tempering. This Indian five spice blend includes cumin, fenugreek, mustard, fennel and nigella seeds. A tsp of panch phoran is enough for this dish.*

**NUTRITIONAL VALUES** (per portion): Energy 230.83 cal, Protein 1.81 gm, Carbohydrate 24.2 gm, Fat 14.78 gm

# PANEER TAKA-TAK

*Paneer cubes are first grilled with flavourful spices and then added to an onion-tomato masala.*

## INGREDIENTS

- 500 g/1 lb paneer
- 2 onions - chopped
- 2 big tomatoes - chopped
- ½ cup tomato puree
- 1 cup yogurt - hang in a muslin cloth for ½ hour
- 1 tsp salt
- ½ tsp red chilli powder
- 2 tbsp cornflour or flour (*maida*)
- 1 tbsp ginger juliennes
- 1 tsp chopped green chillies
- 4 tbsp oil
- ½ tsp cumin seeds

## SPICES

- seeds of 5-6 green cardamoms (*chhoti elaichi*)
- 1 inch stick cinnamon (*dalchini*)
- 4-5 cloves (*laung*)
- ½ tsp carom seeds (*ajwain*)

## METHOD

1. Crush seeds of green cardamoms, cloves, cinnamon stick and carom seeds together in a mortar and pestle. Keep aside.
2. Add the above ground spices, salt, red chilli powder and cornflour to the hung yogurt. Add 2 tbsp oil. Mix well.
3. Cut paneer into 1 inch/2.5 cm pieces or slightly bigger sides. Mix the yogurt mixture nicely with the paneer.
4. Grill the paneer pieces in a hot oven for 5-6 minutes till light golden. Turn side and grill the other side too.
5. At serving time, heat 2 tbsp oil in a pan. Add ½ tsp cumin seeds, when they splutter, add chilli powder and onions. Stir till golden. Add ginger and green chillies.
6. Add tomatoes, tomato puree and ½ tsp salt, stir till oil separates.
7. Add grilled paneer and mix well for 2-3 minutes. Serve.

**TIP:**
*Enjoy a cup of masala tea by boiling water with these crushed spices - ¼" cinnamon, 1 clove and seeds of 1 green cardamom.*

**NUTRITIONAL VALUES** (per portion): Energy 235 cal, Protein 14.39 gm, Carbohydrate 10.65 gm, Fat 15.48 gm

# STUFFED BHINDI

*Serves 4*

*Lady finger or okra as it is called in the west, it cooked whole or cut into small pieces. Initially okra should be cooked without covering till no longer sticky. Later it can be covered and cooked till done.*

## INGREDIENTS

- 250 g/8 oz lady fingers (*bhindi*)
- ½ tsp fennel (*saunf*)
- 1 tsp nigella seeds (*kalaunji*)
- 1 tsp cumin seeds (*jeera*)
- 2 green chillies - whole
- 4 tbsp oil

### STUFFING

- 4 tbsp gramflour (*besan*)
- 4 tsp ground cumin (*jeera*)
- 2 tsp ground coriander (*dhania*)
- 2 tsp fennel (*saunf*) - crushed to a powder
- 2 tsp dry mango powder (*amchoor*)
- 1½ tsp garam masala
- 1½ tsp red chilli powder
- 1½ tsp turmeric powder
- 1 tsp salt, or to taste
- 1 tbsp oil

## METHOD

1. Wash and cut the stalk end of lady fingers. Make a slit length ways in each for the filling.

2. In a mixing bowl put gram flour, red chilli powder, cumin powder, coriander powder, powdered fennel, dry mango powder, garam masala, turmeric powder, salt and 1 tbsp oil. Mix well.

3. Stuff this mixture in each lady finger.

4. Heat 4 tbsp oil in a pan or a big kadhai, add fennel, nigella seeds and cumin seeds, when fennel starts to change colour, add lady fingers and whole green chillies. Stir for 4-5 minutes without covering. Cover with a lid and cook on low heat for about 10 minutes till soft.

5. Uncover and cook lady fingers for about 10 minutes till crisp. Serve hot with roti.

**TIP:**
*Lady fingers should be tender and young, with small seeds. To check this, snap off the pointed end. If it breaks off easily the vegetable is good.*

**NUTRITIONAL VALUES** (per portion): Energy 152 cal, Protein 5.24 gm, Carbohydrate 6.84 gm, Fat 13.81 gm

# LEGUMES & PULSES

The most common version of cooked pulses is 'Dal' which is the main source of proteins in an Indian vegetarian diet. Tempering the same pulses in different ways with different spices makes them different in all the various regions of India. The Southern parts of India relish their pulses tempered with black mustard seeds where as the North Indians prefer to use cumin seeds. Adding a few vegetables to the pulses enhances their taste and nutritive value. Dals can be used whole, split or husked. Whole pulses and other legumes like chickpeas & beans, take longer to cook than split ones.

MOONG DHULI

SKINNED, SPLIT MOONG BEANS

MASOOR DHULI

SKINNED, SPLIT RED LENTILS

URAD DHULI

SKINNED, SPLIT BLACK LENTILS

SAFED/KABULI CHANNE

WHITE CHICKPEAS

RAJMAH

KIDNEY BEANS

# DAL MAKHANI

*Serves 6-8*

*A favourite of the North Indians. Black beans are cooked in butter (makhan) as the name suggests. The addition of a few kidney beans further enhances the taste, although their addition is optional. These black beans, garnished with a white swirl of cream and some fresh coriander are simply superb!*

## INGREDIENTS

- 1 cup (250 g/8 oz) black beans (*saboot urad dal*)
- 2 tbsp red kidney beans (*rajmah*), optional
- 2 tbsp split gram lentils (*channe ki dal*)
- salt to taste
- ½ tsp red chilli powder
- ½ tsp garam masala
- 1 tbsp dry fenugreek leaves (*kasoori methi*)
- 1 tbsp ginger paste
- 1 tbsp garlic paste
- 1 cup tomato puree
- ¼ cup butter
- ½ cup (125 ml/4 oz) cream
- some fresh coriander to garnish

## METHOD

1. Wash the black beans, red kidney beans and gram lentils and soak in enough water for 6-8 hours or overnight.

2. Drain water from the soaked dals. Wash several times, rubbing well, till the water looks clean.

3. Put the drained lentils in a large pan, add 8 cups of water, 2 tbsp butter, ginger and garlic paste. Bring to a boil. Lower the heat to very low, cover and simmer for 2 hours or until cooked. (Ideally, it should be cooked in a slow cooker). Alternatively, add only 5 cups of water and pressure cook to give 2 whistles. Pressure cook on low heat for 25-30 minutes.

4. When the lentils are done, mash them slightly against the sides of the pan with a ladle.

5. Add remaining butter, tomato puree, chilli powder, garam masala, kasoori methi and salt. Simmer, stirring at regular intervals, for 30 minutes.

6. Stir in the cream, keeping aside some for garnishing. Adjust the seasonings. Remove to a bowl, garnish with the remaining cream and fresh coriander. Serve with tandoori roti or parantha.

Step 1

Step 4

**NUTRITIONAL VALUES** (per portion): Energy 217.22 cal, Protein 8.16 gm, Carbohydrate 20.22 gm, Fat 11.39 gm

# MASALA CHANNE

*Chick peas, commonly known as kabuli channe in India, are relished with fried bread called 'Bhaturas'. There are many different ways of cooking channas, but this one is flavoured with black cardamoms and cumin*

## INGREDIENTS

- 200 g/6 oz (1 cup) dried chick peas *(kabuli channe)* or 2½ cups canned chick peas
- 1 tea bag
- 6 tbsp oil
- ½ tsp cumin seeds *(jeera)*
- 2-3 black cardamoms *(moti elaichi)*
- 1 large onion - chopped (¾ cup)
- 2 tomatoes - chopped (1 cup)
- ½ tsp garam masala
- 1 tbsp shredded ginger
- 1 tbsp ground coriander *(dhaniya powder)*
- 1 tsp dry mango powder *(amchoor)*
- ¾ tsp red chilli powder
- salt to taste
- ¼ tsp black salt *(kala namak)*

### GARNISH

- green chillies
- onion rings
- tomato & lemon wedges

## METHOD

1. Cover dried chick peas well with water in a bowl, stand overnight. Drain and rinse with fresh water. Drain again. Add 3-4 cups water and the tea bag. Boil. Simmer till done. Alternately, pressure cook to a whistle. Keep on low heat for 15 minutes. Remove from heat. When no longer hot, remove tea bag.

2. Strain the boiled chick peas, reserving the water.

3. Heat 3 tbsp oil. Add chick peas without the water to the hot oil and stir fry for 5 minutes. Remove from pan and keep the fried chick peas aside.

4. Heat 3 tbsp more oil in a clean pan. Add cardamom pods and cumin. When cumin turns golden brown, add onions and stir fry till onions turn light brown. Add ground coriander, dry mango powder and red chilli powder. Stir till onions turn deep brown, but take care not to burn them.

5. Add tomatoes, garam masala and shredded ginger. Cook till tomatoes get well blended and oil surfaces. Add the fried chick peas and stir fry for 2-3 minutes. Gradually add the liquid of the boiled chick peas, adding a little at a time. Add black salt and salt. When all the liquid is over, simmer on low heat for 15-20 minutes.

6. Serve garnished with slit green chillies, onion rings, tomato and lemon wedges.

Step 2

Step 3

**NOTE:**
If you are using canned chick peas, you may just jump step 1 and 2. Continue further.

**NUTRITIONAL VALUES** (per portion): Energy 264.00 cal, Protein 6.09 gm, Carbohydrate 22.07 gm, Fat 16.79 gm

# SAMBHAR

*Sambar is a hot & sour dal of Southern India. It features three main ingredients — toor dal (pigeon peas), tamarind pulp, and a special spice powder called sambhar powder. The tamarind pulp may be increased if you like it more sour.*

## INGREDIENTS

- 1 cup mixed vegetables of your choice - beans, potato, lady's finger, brinjal, capsicum, carrots
- ½ cup toor/arhar dal (*yellow lentils*)
- 2 green chillies - slit lengthways
- 1 onion - cut into slices (½ cup)
- 3 tsp sambhar powder (see page 29)
- a pinch of turmeric (*haldi*) powder
- lemon-sized ball of tamarind (*imli*) or 1 tbsp tamarind pulp
- salt to taste
- 1 tomato - chopped finely

## TEMPERING

- 2 tbsp oil
- ½ tsp mustard seeds (*sarson*)
- 2 pinches asafoetida (*hing*) powder
- ¼ tsp fenugreek seeds (*methi dana*)
- ½ tsp cumin seeds (*jeera*)
- 1 dry red chilli
- a few curry leaves

## METHOD

1. Wash and boil yellow lentils with 2½ cups water. Reduce heat, cover and simmer till well blended. Alternately, pressure cook for 10 minutes on ow heat after the first whistle.

2. Soak tamarind in 1 cup of hot water and extract pulp.

3. Cut beans into 1 inch/2.5 cm long pieces, potato, brinjal and capsicum into 1 inch/2.5 cm cubes, carrot into round thick slices, leaving lady fingers whole.

4. Heat oil. Add all the ingredients of the tempering together. When the mustard seeds splutter, add the sliced onions and cook till golden. Add slit green chillies and the chopped vegetables. Fry for 3-4 minutes.

5. Add the tamarind pulp, salt, turmeric and sambhar powder. Cover and simmer on low heat till the vegetables are tender.

6. Add the cooked lentils and chopped tomato. Boil and then simmer for 5 to 10 minutes on low heat till everything blends. Serve hot with rice.

Step 5

**NUTRITIONAL VALUES** (per portion): Energy 139.88 cal, Protein 5.28 gm, Carbohydrate 18.46 gm, Fat 5.09 gm

# DHABE KI DAL

*A combination of five lentils are used to prepare this dal delicacy.*

## INGEDIENTS

### FIVE DALS (WASH ALL DALS AND SOAK TOGETHER FOR 2 HOURS)

- ¼ cup saboot moong dal (green)
- ¼ cup saboot masoor dal (brown)
- ¼ cup saboot urad dal (black)
- ¼ cup channa dal (yellow)
- ¼ cup toor dal (yellow)

### OTHER INGREDIENTS

- 2 tbsp ghee
- 1 tsp black cumin seeds (*shah jeera*)
- ½ onion - chopped
- 2 tsp ground coriander (*dhaniya*)
- ½ tsp red chilli powder
- ½ tsp turmeric powder (*haldi*)
- 1 tsp salt, or to taste

### TEMPERING

- 3 tbsp butter/ghee
- 1 tomato - chopped finely
- ½ cup yogurt - beat well till smooth
- ½ tsp garam masala
- seeds of 1 black cardamom (*moti elaichi*) - crushed
- ½ tsp red chilli powder
- ¼ cup green coriander - chopped

## METHOD

1. Heat ghee in a heavy bottomed pan. Add black cumin and saute over medium heat until they begin to crackle.
2. Add onion, saute until light brown.
3. Drain the dals and add to the onion. Stir for 4-5 minutes on low heat.
4. Add coriander powder, red chilli, turmeric powder and salt.
5. Add about 5 cups water & bring to a boil. Reduce heat & remove scum. Cover and simmer for about ½ hour, until lentils are done.
6. To prepare the tempering, melt butter in a kadhai, add tomatoes, yogurt and garam masala, stir over medium heat until the fat leaves the sides. Add crushed seeds of black cardamom. Stir for a few seconds. Add red chilli powder.
7. Add the cooked lentils and stir for 3-4 minutes. Remove to a bowl, garnish with coriander and serve hot.

### MOONG SABUT

WHOLE MOONG BEANS

### MASOOR SABUT

WHOLE RED LENTILS

### URAD SABUT

WHOLE BLACK LENTILS

### CHANNE KI DAL

GRAM LENTILS

### ARHAR/TOOR

YELLOW LENTILS

**TIP:**
*Traditional house holds of India, even today use butter or ghee for tempering dals. Oil can be substituted for health reasons.*

**NUTRITIONAL VALUES** (per portion): Energy 326.10 cal, Protein 8.72 gm, Carbohydrate 25.79 gm, Fat 20.89 gm

# CHICKEN & MUTTON

Curries as well as dry preparations of meat are popular. Chicken is the most popular amongst all meat preparations in India. Butter chicken, which has succulent pieces of chicken in a fragrant tomato curry cooked in butter is the most common dish ordered in Indian restaurants. Tandoori Chicken, a dry preparation in which chicken is marinated with herbs and spices and later barbecued in an oven, makes a meal very interesting.

Mutton, which is goat meat, is also relished by many. Mutton dishes of Hyderabad and Kashmir are very popular.

# TANDOORI CHICKEN

*Serves 4*

*An all time favourite! A must on the Indian menu in restaurants. The two different marinades make it taste special. However, if you are short of time, marinate the chicken with all the ingredients of the first and second marinade together at one time.*

## INGREDIENTS

- 1 chicken (750 g/1½ lb) - cut into 4 or 8 pieces
- 2 tsp tandoori masala (page 29) - to sprinkle

### FIRST MARINADE

- 1½ tbsp lemon juice
- 1 tbsp ginger-garlic paste
- 1 tsp chilli powder
- 1 tsp salt

### SECOND MARINADE

- ½ cup thick yogurt (*dahi*)
- 2 tbsp thick cream
- 1 onion - grated & squeezed
- 1 tbsp garlic paste
- 1 tsp ginger paste
- ½ tsp rock salt (*kala namak*)
- 1 tsp garam masala
- 1 tsp tandoori masala
- 1 tbsp dry fenugreek leaves (*kasuri methi*) - crushed
- few drops of orange red food colour
- ¼ tsp salt, or to taste

## METHOD

1. Wash and pat dry the chicken pieces. Make deep incisions — two incisions on the breast, two on the thighs and two on the drumsticks too.

2. Mix lemon juice, ginger-garlic paste, salt & chilli powder and rub well on the chicken pieces, and also inside the incisions. Keep the marinated chicken aside for 30 minutes.

3. In a bowl mix all ingredients of the second marinade and marinate the chicken with it. Keep the chicken aside for 3-4 hours to marinate.

4. Heat a gas tandoor (the heat should be minimum) or an electric oven to 180°C/350°F. Place the chicken on the grill or wire rack (in the oven place a tray underneath the chicken to collect the drippings).

5. Grill for 8-10 minutes. Brush pieces with oil. Turn the pieces and grill for another 8-10 minutes, till the chicken is dry and well cooked. Remove to a serving platter. Sprinkle some tandoori masala. Serve hot with onion rings and lemon wedges.

Step 4

# BUTTER CHICKEN

*Chicken cooked in a fragrant red coloured sauce made in butter. Relished by almost everyone!*

## INGREDIENTS

- 1 tandoori chicken
  (page 106) - cut into 8 pieces

### GRAVY

- 500 g/1 lb tomatoes
  - boiled in hot water for
  3-4 minutes and ground
  to a puree
- 50 g/2 oz salted butter
- 1 tbsp ginger-garlic paste
- ¼ cup cashews - soaked in
  hot water for 15 minutes
- ¼ tsp degi mirch or paprika
- ½ cup milk, approx.
- 100 g/3 oz thin fresh cream
  (½ cup)
- ½ tsp garam masala
- salt to taste
- ¼ tsp sugar
- 1 tsp tandoori masala
  (see page 29)
- 1 bay leaf *(tej patta)*

## METHOD

1. Soak cashews in hot water for 15 minutes. Drain and grind to a very fine paste with a little water.

2. Melt butter in nonstick pan. Add a bay leaf. Wait for a few seconds. Add ginger-garlic paste, cook until liquid evaporates and the paste just changes colour. Add freshly pureed tomatoes, cook until the puree turns absolutely dry and fat separates.

3. Add cashew paste, stir for a few seconds. Add 2 tbsp cream. Add paprika or degi mirch to give a bright red colour, (a few drops of orange red food colour can also be added). Cook on medium heat till fat separates.

4. Add enough water (about 1 cup) to get a thick curry. Mix well. Return to heat. Bring to a boil, stirring constantly. Simmer for 5-7 minutes till the gravy turns to a bright red colour and fat surfaces.

5. Remove from heat and let it cool slightly. Stir in rest of the cream, and some milk to get the right consistency of the gravy. Add garam masala, tandoori masala, salt and sugar to taste.

6. Add tandoori chicken. Give one or two quick boils on low heat and heat through. Remove from heat. Garnish with 1 tbsp of fresh cream and slit green chillies. Serve hot with nan or paranthas.

Step 5

**TIP:**
*Instead of using tandoori chicken for this recipe, you can cook chicken in a kadhai also. Marinate chicken with the same ingredients as for tandoori chicken and cook in butter in a kadhai instead of an oven.*

**NUTRITIONAL VALUES** (per portion): Energy 234.92 cal, Protein 34.58 gm, Carbohydrate 3.88 gm, Fat 8.46 gm

# RARA MEAT

*It's a meaty double, mutton pieces and mince together.*

## INGREDIENTS

- 250 gms mutton
- 100 gm mutton mince (*keema*)
- ¾ cup yogurt - beaten well till smooth
- 1 tsp salt
- 5 tbsp ghee/oil
- 2 black cardamoms (*moti elaichi*)
- 1" stick cinnamon (*dalchini*)
- 1 bay leaf (*tej patta*)
- 1 big onion - finely chopped (1 cup)
- 1 tsp ginger paste
- 1 tsp garlic paste
- 2 big tomatoes - finely chopped (1 cup)
- 1 tsp red chilli powder
- ½ tsp turmeric (*haldi*) powder
- 1 tsp coriander powder
- ¾ tsp garam masala powder

## GARNISHING

- some fresh chopped coriander leaves

## METHOD

1. Whisk yogurt. Add salt and mutton pieces and let it marinate for 1-1½ hours.
2. Heat ghee/oil in a pressure cooker.
3. Add cinnamon, black cardamoms and bay leaf. Fry for few seconds.
4. Add onion. Fry till light brown.
5. Add ginger and garlic paste, turmeric powder, coriander powder, garam masala and tomatoes. Cook till tomatoes are soft and well mixed.
6. Add mutton pieces and mutton keema along with the marinade and cook till oil separates.
7. Add 1¼ cups water. Mix well. Close the cooker and give 2 whistles. Reduce heat and keep for 5 minutes. Remove from fire.
8. When pressure drops, open cooker and check tenderness of mutton. If done, stir on low heat till oil/ghee separates. Sprinkle fresh coriander on top and serve hot with rotis.

**TIP:**
*Cooking the mutton on low heat for 40 minutes without the pressure cooker adds more flavour to the dish.*

**NUTRITIONAL VALUES** (per portion): Energy ??? cal, Protein ?? gm, Carbohydrate ?? gm, Fat ??? gm

# GOAN CHICKEN XACUTI

*The word xacuti is pronounced 'shakuti'. An all-time favourite of Goan food lovers, it is a sell-out in most Goan restaurants.*

## INGREDIENTS

- 750 g/1½ lb chicken - cut into 12 pieces
- 4 tbsp oil
- 2 medium sized onions - finely chopped
- 2 cups water
- 1 tbsp tamarind (*imli*) pulp
- ¼ tsp nutmeg (*jaiphal*) - grated

### DRY ROASTED MASALA PASTE

- 4-6 flakes of garlic
- 1 cup grated fresh coconut
- 2" stick of cinnamon (*dalchini*)
- 6 cloves (*laung*)
- 4 dry red chillies (*sookhi lal mirch*)
- ½ tsp turmeric powder (*haldi*)
- 2 tbsp poppy seeds (*khus khus*)
- 1 tsp carom seeds (*ajwain*)
- ½ tsp cumin seeds (*jeera*)
- 10 peppercorns (*saboot kali mirch*)
- 1 tsp fennel seeds (*saunf*)
- 4 star anise (*chakri phool*)
- 1½ tbsp coriander seeds (*saboot dhaniya*)
- 1 tsp salt

## METHOD

1. Dry roast in a pan, coconut, garlic, cinnamon, cloves, whole red chillies, turmeric powder, poppy seeds, carom seeds, cumin seeds, peppercorns, fennel seeds, star anise and coriander seeds for 1-2 minutes. Remove. Cool. Grind to a paste with ¾ cup of water. Add salt.

2. Heat oil in a kadhai/wok, add onions. Stir till golden brown.

3. Add the prepared masala paste and cook for 2 minutes.

4. Add the chicken pieces and saute for 7- 8 minutes.

5. Add 2 cups of water. Bring to a boil. Add salt if required. Lower heat and cook covered for 5 minutes.

6. Add tamarind pulp, grated nutmeg and mix well. Cook for a minute. Serve hot with steamed rice.

**TIP:**
*Mushroom xacuti is a wonderful variation for the vegetarians. Use 500 gm/1 lb button mushroom for this recipe.*

**NUTRITIONAL VALUES** (per portion): Energy 289 cal, Protein 34.21 gm, Carbohydrate 3.75 gm, Fat 14.6 gm

# ROGAN JOSH

*A spicy thin mutton curry from Kashmir, cooked with fennel seeds and ground dry ginger.*

## INGREDIENTS

- 500 g/1 lb lamb (*mutton*)
- ½ cup yogurt (*dahi*)
- ¼ tsp asafoetida (*hing*)
- 4 tbsp oil
- 1 onion - ground to a paste (½ cup)
- salt to taste

### GRIND TO A FINE POWDER

- 2 tsp fennel seeds (*saunf*)
- seeds of 3 brown cardamoms (*moti elaichi*)
- 1 tsp cumin seeds (*jeera*)
- 2 cloves (*laung*)
- 3-4 dry, red chillies
- 1 tbsp dry ginger powder (*sonth*)

## METHOD

1. Wash and pat dry mutton on a kitchen towel.
2. Heat oil in a pressure cooker or a deep pan. Add asafoetida powder.
3. Add dry meat and stir fry till the mutton turns dry and all the water evaporates. Stir fry further till the mutton turns golden brown and gives a well fried look.
4. Add onion paste and stir fry for 3-4 minutes on medium heat.
5. Mix the yogurt with the freshly ground spices and add it to the mutton. Add salt. Stir fry for 5-7 minutes till the yogurt blends well and turns dry.
6. Add 2 cups of water, pressure cook to give 2 whistles. Reduce heat and pressure cook further for 5 minutes. If you are not using a pressure cooker, add extra water and cook covered on low heat till the mutton gets done. Check for tenderness. Serve hot with rice.

Step 1

**TIP:**
*If you cannot grind the spices to a fine powder, sift the ground spices through a fine strainer to get a fine powder.*

**NUTRITIONAL VALUES** (per portion): Energy 297.50 cal, Protein 27.53 gm, Carbohydrate 0.75 gm, Fat 20.50 gm

# KADHAI MURG

*The kadhai masala has coriander and fenugreek, both in their herb as well as spice form.*

## INGREDIENTS

- 1 medium sized (750 g/ 1½ lb) chicken - cut into 12 pieces
- 6-7 tbsp oil
- 1 tbsp coriander seeds (*saboot dhaniya*)
- 3 whole, dry red chillies
- ½ tsp fenugreek seeds (*methi dana*)
- 3 onions - finely chopped
- 15-20 flakes garlic - crushed & chopped
- 1 inch piece ginger - crushed to a paste (1 tbsp)
- 3 tomatoes - finely chopped
- ¾ cup ready-made tomato puree or 1 cup homemade puree
- 1 tbsp dry fenugreek greens (*kasoori methi*)
- 1 tsp red chilli powder
- 1 tsp ground coriander powder
- 2 tsp salt, or to taste
- ¼ tsp dry mango powder (*amchoor*)
- ½ tsp garam masala
- ½ cup chopped green coriander
- 1 capsicum - cut into slices
- 1 inch piece ginger - cut into match sticks
- 1-2 green chillies - cut into long slices
- ½ cup cream

## METHOD

1. Roast coriander seeds in a pan, till they just starts to change colour. Do not make them brown. Remove from fire.
2. Crush the coriander seeds on a rolling board and pin (*chakla-belan*) to crush the seeds. Keep aside.
3. Heat oil in a kadhai. Reduce heat. Add fenugreek seeds, coriander seeds and whole red chillies and stir for a few seconds till fenugreek seeds turns golden.
4. Add onion and cook on medium heat till light brown.
5. Add garlic and stir for 1 minute. Add ginger paste.
6. Add red chilli powder and coriander powder. Add 1 tbsp water.
7. Add chicken and stir for 10 minutes on medium flame, stirring well so that chicken attains a nice golden colour.
8. Add finely chopped tomatoes. Add salt, dry mango powder and garam masala. Stir till dry. Cover and cook for 5-7 minutes or till tender, stirring occasionally.
9. Add *kasoori methi*, tomato puree and chopped green coriander. Cook for 5 minutes.
10. Add the capsicum, ginger match sticks & green chilli slices. Mix well.
11. Reduce heat. Add cream. Mix well for 2-3 minutes and remove from fire. Serve hot.

**TIP:**
*When buying chicken, see that it is pink in colour. A dark coloured chicken is always stale. Also if the chicken is too big it is very fibrous. Choose a small broiler chicken with tender meat.*

**NUTRITIONAL VALUES** (per portion): Energy 289 cal, Protein 34.21 gm, Carbohydrate 3.75 gm, Fat 14.6 gm

# FISH & SEA FOOD

The healthy image of fish has prompted us to regard it as the obvious alternative to meat. Not only is fish delicious but highly nutritious as well. Fish can be barbecued, fried or put into a curry. The cooking time of fish is much less in comparison to poultry. If over cooked, the fish is no longer moist and succulent. It turns dry and does not taste good. India offers a large variety of fish and prawns, each with a distinct flavour and texture. Diversity in climate, cultures, social habits and varied locations offer a range of styles and cooking methods.

# FRIED FISH

*A popular way to serve pan fried fish. Tartar sauce, although not traditionally Indian, is relished with this Indian preparation of fish. You may have it even with ordinary tomato ketchup.*

## INGREDIENTS

- 500 g/1 lb white fish fillet - without bones
- 1 tbsp lemon juice
- some dry bread crumbs

### MARINADE

- 1 tbsp ginger paste
- ½ tsp salt
- ½ tsp ground black pepper
- ½ tsp red chilli powder
- 1 tsp tomato sauce
- 1 egg white
- a few coriander leaves - chopped

### TARTAR SAUCE (OPTIONAL)

- ½ cup mayonnaise
- ¼ cup brown vinegar
- 1 tbsp very finely chopped cucumber
- 1 tbsp very finely chopped onion

## METHOD

1. Rub some lemon juice on the fillets and wash fish well. Transfer it to a kitchen towel and pat dry. Cut into 2" pieces.

2. Mix all ingredients of the marinade together in a small bowl. Transfer fish to a plate and rub marinade on the fish. Keep aside for 30 minutes.

3. At serving time, press the fish on bread crumbs such that they coat the fish. Fry on medium heat till golden. Drain on absorbent paper. Serve with tomato ketchup or tartar sauce given below.

4. For tartar sauce, soak onion and cucumber in vinegar for 30 minutes. Strain the cucumber and onion to drain out the vinegar. Press gently to remove any excess liquid. Gently mix the cucumber and onion into the mayonnaise. Serve with fried fish.

Step 2

**TIP:**
*A little ajwain (carom seeds) added to the marinade, gives the fried fish a distinctly delicious taste.*

**NUTRITIONAL VALUES** (per portion): Energy 211 cal, Protein 13 gm, Carbohydrate 15 gm, Fat 11 gm

# BENGALI FISH CURRY

*Serves 4*

*A flavourful thin curry, seasoned with ground spices like ginger, cumin, coriander, chilli and turmeric. Enjoy it with rice.*

## INGREDIENTS

- 400 g/1 lb boneless fish fillet - cut into 2" pieces
- 1 tsp turmeric (*haldi*)
- ¾ tsp salt
- 5 tbsp mustard oil or any cooking oil for frying
- ½ tsp onion seeds (*kalaunji*)
- 6 dry, whole red chillies
- 4 bay leaves (*tej patta*)
- 1 big onion - chopped
- ½ cup ready made tomato puree
- 4 whole green chillies

### SPICE PASTE (MIX TOGETHER)

- 1 tsp ground coriander seeds (*dhaniya powder*)
- ½ tsp ground cumin (*jeera powder*)
- ½ tsp finely grated ginger
- 1 tsp ground turmeric (*haldi*)
- a pinch of red chilli powder
- 1 tsp salt
- 6 tbsp water

## METHOD

1. To remove fishy odour, rub the fish well with turmeric and salt and keep aside for 10-15 minutes.

2. Heat oil in a non-stick frying pan over medium flame. If you are using mustard oil, let it smoke a little. Remove from fire. Cool and reheat. Now put in the fish pieces and brown lightly on all sides without cooking them through, for about 1 minute on each side.

3. Gently lift the fish out of the oil and place it on a plate. Keep aside.

4. Combine all ingredients of the spice paste in a small bowl. Keep aside.

5. Heat remaining oil in the pan. Add onion seeds, dry red chillies and bay leaves. Stir for a few seconds.

6. Add onion and cook till light brown.

7. Add the spice paste. Stir. Add tomato puree. Stir and fry for about 2-3 minutes till oil separate.

8. Add 2 cups of water. Give one boil. Simmer for 3-4 minutes.

9. Add fish and green chillies. Simmer over medium heat for 2 minutes till the fish is cooked. Serve

**TIP:**
*When buying fish, press it with the thumb. If if forms a depression and does not spring back, the fish is not fresh.*

**NUTRITIONAL VALUES** (per portion): Energy 269 cal, Protein 16.2 gm, Carbohydrate 3.45 gm, Fat 21.05 gm

# TANDOORI FISH

*Barbecued fish — a delicious & popular fish preparation.*

## INGREDIENTS

- 500 g/1 lb fish - cut into thick fingers
- 2 tbsp gram flour *(besan)*
- 1 tbsp lemon juice
- chaat masala to sprinkle (optional, page 29)

## 1ST MARINADE

- 2 tbsp lemon juice, salt & red chilli powder to taste

## 2ND MARINADE

- 1 tsp ginger paste
- 2 tsp garlic paste
- 2-3 tbsp thick yogurt
- ½ tsp carom seeds *(ajwain)*
- 1 tbsp dried fenugreek leaves *(kasoori methi)* - crushed
- a few drops of orange-red food colour
- 2 tbsp oil

## METHOD

1. Rub the fish with gram flour and lemon juice to remove the fishy odour. Wash well and remove on a kitchen towel and pat dry.

2. Ist Marinade: Place the fish in a vessel, rub with lemon juice, salt and chilli powder. Keep the marinated fish aside for 30 minutes.

3. 2nd Marinade: later add garlic, ginger paste, yogurt, carom seeds, dried fenugreek leaves, colour and oil to the fish. Rub well. Marinate for at least 30 minutes or till the time of grilling.

4. Grill in a medium hot oven. Baste with butter in between. Grill till done. Sprinkle some chaat masala and serve.

Step 1

**TIP:**
*You may fry the fish instead of grilling. To fry, sprinkle some cornflour on the marinated fish to give a dry coating. If the cornflour gets wet, roll the fish pieces in dry cornflour once again before shallow frying.*

**NUTRITIONAL VALUES** (per portion): Energy 166.8 cal, Protein 16.2 gm, Carbohydrate 3.45 gm, Fat 9.8 gm

# PRAWN CURRY

*Serves 4-6*

*A delicious, spicy prawn curry with coconut milk.*

## INGREDIENTS

- 250 g/8 oz prawns - shelled, with tails intact
- 2 tbsp oil
- 1 tsp red chilli-garlic paste
- ½ tsp ground turmeric
- 2 cups coconut milk
- ½ tsp salt, or to taste
- ½ tsp sugar
- 4-5 cherry tomatoes or 125 g/4 oz regular tomatoes - cut into 1 inch/2.5 cm pieces
- 1-2 tbsp lemon juice or to taste

## GARNISH

- 1-2 green/red chillies - chopped
- some green coriander leaves

## METHOD

1. Heat oil. Add chilli-garlic paste and turmeric. Fry for a minute on low heat till oil separates.

2. Add ¾ cup coconut milk. Boil, stirring constantly. Simmer for 5-7 minutes. Add salt and sugar. Add the rest of the coconut milk. Boil for 3-4 minutes.

3. Add prawns and tomatoes. Cook for 4-5 minutes till prawns are cooked and the gravy becomes thick. Add lemon juice. Mix.

4. Garnish with chopped chillies and coriander leaves. Serve hot with rice.

Step 1

Step 2

**NUTRITIONAL VALUES** (per portion): Energy 232.42 cal, Protein 9.56 gm, Carbohydrate 5.43 gm, Fat 19.12 gm

# RICE & BREADS

Indian Basmati rice is very popular for it's fragrance and flavour. Rice is cooked with spices and vegetables or meat to create exotic pulaos and biryaanis. Most Indian homes serve freshly cooked flat breads (rotis), a luxury almost all Indian men like to indulge in. The lady of the house derives great pleasure in serving her man, hot rotis, one at a time, straight off the cooking stove. A dollop of butter or ghee smeared on these flat breads, makes them just wonderful!

# SPINACH - CARROT RICE

*Serves 4*

*A healthy combination of spinach and rice! It's not only delicious, but the green spinach ribbons scattered on white rice makes it very tempting. The carrot shreds enhance the look further.*

## INGREDIENTS

- 1 cup basmati rice - soaked for about 30 minutes
- 350 g/11 oz spinach *(palak)* - discard stems & cut leaves into thin strips (2 cups)
- 2 carrots - grated (1 cup)
- 4 tbsp oil
- ½ tsp fennel seeds *(saunf)*
- 2 brown cardamoms *(moti elaichi)*
- 1 stick cinnamon *(dalchini)*
- 2 cloves *(laung)*
- 1 onion - sliced finely (½ cup)
- 1½ tsp salt, or to taste
- ¼ tsp red chilli powder or paprika
- 2 tsp lemon juice

## METHOD

1. Soak rice for about 30 minutes.
2. Heat oil in a large, heavy bottomed pan. Add fennel seeds, cardamoms, cinnamon and cloves. Wait till fennel seeds just change colour.
3. Add onions and stir fry till transparent. Add spinach and grated carrots. Stir fry for 1 minute.
4. Drain the water from the rice and add to the spinach. Add salt and red chilli powder. Stir for a minute. Add 2 cups water and lemon juice. Stir gently to mix well.
5. Boil. Reduce heat and cook covered, for 12-15 minutes or until the rice is done. Fluff it up with a fork to separate the grains. Serve hot with a refreshing raita (yogurt).

Step 2

Step 3

**NUTRITIONAL VALUES** (per portion): Energy 273.96 cal, Protein 4.03 gm, Carbohydrate 28.83 gm, Fat 15.80 gm

# CAULIFLOWER PARANTHAS

*These are pan fried flat breads which are stuffed with a spicy cauliflower filling. In India we relish them with just plain yogurt and some pickle or a chutney, during the winter months. My son, Anurag, likes to add a dollop of butter on the paranthas and that's a treat for him!*

## INGREDIENTS

### DOUGH

- 2 cups whole wheat flour (atta)
- ½ tsp salt
- about ¾ cups water to knead

### FILLING

- 2 cups grated cauliflower
- 1 tsp salt
- ½ tsp garam masala
- ½ tsp red chilli powder
- 1 inch/2.5 cm piece ginger - grated finely
- 2-3 tbsp chopped, fresh coriander
- 1 green chilli - deseeded and chopped finely
- oil or butter for frying

## METHOD

1. Mix salt and whole wheat flour in a shallow pan or a food processor. Add enough water to get a dough of rolling consistency. Knead well till smooth. Cover and keep aside for at least 30 minutes.

2. To prepare the filling, add all ingredients to the grated cauliflower and mix well. Keep aside for 15 minutes. Squeeze the cauliflower well after 15 minutes to drain out the excess water.

3. Make 2 marble sized balls of the dough. Roll out each ball into very thin rounds. Spread some filling on one rolled out dough and cover with the other round. Press the edges well to join.

4. Carefully pick up the parantha and put it on a hot griddle or a frying pan. When the underside is cooked, turn to cook the other side. Smear some oil or butter on the parantha. Trickle some oil on the sides too, around the edges. Turn the parantha and press, especially on the edges with a flat spoon, till golden patches appear on the underside. Similarly make other paranthas. Serve with plain yogurt and some pickle or chutney.

Step 3

**TIP:**
*A pinch of carom seeds (ajwain) can be added to the dough for extra flavour.*

**NUTRITIONAL VALUES** (per portion): Energy 271.00 cal, Protein 9.00 gm, Carbohydrate 38.50 gm, Fat 9.00 gm

# MINTY CHICKEN PULAO

*Serves 6*

*Rice cooked with chicken and flavoured with fresh mint.*

## INGREDIENTS

- 2 cups basmati rice - cleaned & soaked in water for 30 minutes
- 8 pieces chicken of 2 inch/5 cm size
- ½ cup mint (*pudina*) leaves - finely chopped
- 4 tbsp oil or ghee
- ½ tsp black cumin seeds (*shah jeera*)
- 1 bay leaf (*tej patta*)
- 2 onions - finely sliced (1 cup)
- 2 whole green chillies
- 2 tomatoes - finely chopped (1 cup)
- ½ tsp chilli powder
- 1 tsp garam masala
- 1½ tsp salt or to taste
- a few strands saffron - soaked in milk, optional

### BOIL TOGETHER

- 5 cups water
- 1 cinnamon (*dalchini*) stick
- 4 cloves (*laung*)
- 4 black cardamoms (*moti elaichi*)
- 1 inch/2.5 cm piece ginger - chopped
- 1 tsp salt

## METHOD

1. Boil 5 cups of water with salt, whole spices and ginger. Add chicken and cook until chicken turns just tender. Remove from heat, strain and keep aside the chicken pieces and the stock separately. Discard the whole spices and ginger.

2. Heat oil or ghee in a large, heavy bottomed pan. Add black cumin seeds and a bay leaf. After 30 seconds, add sliced onions and fry until golden brown. Add green chillies.

3. Add chicken pieces, ½ tsp salt, chopped tomato and mint leaves. Sauté until chicken turns light brown. Add the red chilli powder and garam masala.

4. Add 4 cups of chicken stock. Add the drained rice. Add 1 tsp salt and mix well. Bring to a boil, cover and cook on low heat until all the water is absorbed and the rice is done.

5. Sprinkle soaked saffron and fluff lightly with a fork.

6. Serve hot with a refreshing raita.

**TIP:**
*At step 4, after adding salt, it is a good idea to taste the water. You may add a little more if it seems less.*

**NUTRITIONAL VALUES** (per portion): Energy 288.90 cal, Protein 26.86 gm, Carbohydrate 26.75 gm, Fat 8.25 gm

# NAAN

*Naans are oblong oven baked flat breads. Traditionally they are baked in a clay oven called 'tandoor' but I have prepared them in an electric oven with equal success.*

## INGREDIENTS

- 500 g/1 lb plain flour (*maida*)
- 1 tsp salt
- 1 tsp baking powder
- 1 egg
- ½ cup yogurt
- ½ -¾ cup milk, approx.
- 1 tsp nigella seeds (*kalaunji*)

## METHOD

1. Sift together flour, salt and baking powder.
2. Make a well in the sifted flour. Add egg in the well and mix well. Add yogurt and mix well.
3. Add about ½ cup milk to the sifted ingredients and knead into a soft dough, using more milk if required.
4. Cover the dough with plastic wrap or moist cloth. Keep the dough covered in a warm place for 6-8 hours or overnight.
5. To serve, make balls. Roll out thinly. Brush the surface with some water. Sprinkle some nigella seeds. Stretch lightly.
6. Cook in a tandoor or a preheated oven at 250ºC/450ºF for 3-4 minutes till black patches appear.

**TIP:**
*An electric tandoor works better for making Naans. Cover the tray with aluminium foil and then place the Naans on it for baking. This prevents the Naans from sticking to the tray. Alternately, spray the tray with no-stick cooking spray.*

**NUTRITIONAL VALUES** (per portion): Energy 254.23 cal, Protein 6.94 gm, Carbohydrate 46.25 gm, Fat 4.57 gm

# SUBZ BIRYAANI

*Serves 6*

*The term biryaani is used to define a fragrant rice preparation which was very popular in the Moghul era.*

## INGREDIENTS

### RICE

- 2 cups (250 gms) basmati rice - washed and kept in the strainer for 30 minutes
- 4-5 green cardamoms (*chhoti elaichi*), 2 bay leaves (*tej patta*), 5-6 cloves (*laung*)
- 3 tsp salt, 1 tbsp lemon juice
- 10 cups water

### VEGETABLES

- 2 thin carrots - peeled and cut into cubes, 20 french beans - cut into ¼" pieces
- ½ of a small cauliflower - cut into small florets, ½ cup peas

### MIX TOGETHER

- 1 cup yogurt - hang for 15 minutes in muslin cloth
- 1 tbsp mint - chopped finely
- 1 tbsp coriander - chopped
- 2-3 drops kewra essence or ½ tsp ruh kewra, ½ tsp salt

### CRUSH SPICES TOGETHER

- ½ tsp black cumin (*shah jeera*), 3-4 blades mace (*javetri*)
- seeds of 1 black cardamom (*moti elaichi*), 1 stick of cinnamon (*dalchini*)

### TO SEAL

- aluminium foil and dough

### OTHER INGREDIENTS

- 4-5 tbsp melted ghee or oil
- 8-10 almonds - split into two pieces, 1 tbsp raisins
- 2 large onions - sliced
- 3 tsp ginger-garlic paste
- 1 tsp red chilli pd., 1½ tsp salt
- ½ tsp turmeric (*haldi*)
- a few mint leaves
- seeds of 4 green cardamom (*chhoti elaichi*) - crushed to a powder, 1 tbsp melted ghee

## METHOD

1. Wash rice several times. Strain. Let it be in the strainer for 30 minutes. (Do not soak).

2. Boil 10 cups water with all ingredients given under rice - green cardamoms, cloves, bay leaves, salt and lemon juice.

3. When the water boils, throw in the rice. Stir. Boil just for 4-5 minutes so that the rice is a little chewy and not fully soft.

4. Remove from fire. If you find the grains too hard, let them be in hot water for 2 minutes. Strain in a big steel strainer or a colander. Run a fork frequently in the rice to separate the grains of rice. Let the rice be in the strainer for 10 minutes to drain out all the water. Now spread rice in a big tray on a cloth. Remove whole spices from the cooked rice and discard them.

5. Heat ghee or oil. Add almonds and raisins. Stir for a few seconds. Remove from oil and keep aside for topping.

6. Add onions and stir till rich brown. Remove half onion and keep aside for garnish. Reduce heat. Add crushed spices, ginger-garlic paste, turmeric powder, chilli powder and salt. Mix.

7. Add vegetables and stir for 2 minutes. Cook, stirring on low heat till the vegetables are just done or crisp-tender. Do not over cook. Remove from fire. Add the yogurt mix.

8. To assemble the biryani, take a *handi*. Grease it. Spread 1/3 of the rice in the dish.

9. Spread half of the vegetables over the rice. Put ½ the remaining rice on the vegetables. Do not mix.

10. Repeat vegetable layer using all the vegetable.

11. Spread remaining rice. Sprinkle cardamom powder and 1 tbsp of melted ghee over the rice. Put a few mint leaves on the rice.

12. Sprinkle browned onions, almonds and raisins. Cover with foil.

13. Take a big ball of dough, roll it into a long strip.

14. Cover the *handi* with a foil nicely, pressing the edges well. Seal the end of the *handi* by pressing the dough strip on the foil, sticking it with the *handi*.

15. Keep the *handi* on very low heat for 10-12 minutes. You can keep a griddle (*tawa*) underneath the *handi* to reduce the heat. Serve hot.

**NUTRITIONAL VALUES** (per portion): Energy 259.31 cal, Protein 4.69 gm, Carbohydrate 30.41 gm, Fat 13.18 gm

# BHATURA

*Serves 4*

*These are deep fried breads, which puff up on frying. The semolina makes it crisp, so these breads are crisp on the outside and soft from inside. These are mostly served with masala chick peas.*

## INGREDIENTS

- 250 g/8 oz (2 cups) plain flour (*maida*)
- 100 g/3 oz (¾ cup) semolina (*suji*)
- ½ tsp baking soda
- ½ tsp salt
- 1 tsp sugar
- ½ cup yogurt (*dahi*) (approx.)
- oil for deep frying

## METHOD

1. Soak semolina for 15 minutes in water, which is just enough to cover it.
2. Sift salt, baking soda and flour. Add sugar, semolina and yogurt to the sifted flour. Knead with some warm water to make a smooth dough of rolling consistency. Brush the dough with oil. Keep covered in a warm place for 3-4 hours.
3. At serving time, make 8-10 balls. Roll each ball to an oblong shape. Pull from one side to get a pointed tip.
4. Heat oil. Deep fry bhaturas in medium hot oil. Remove from oil before they turn brown.
5. Serve with masala channas give on page 98.

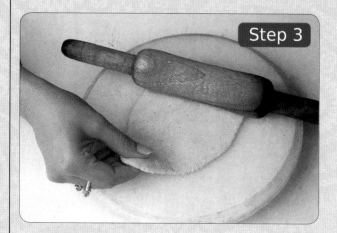

Step 3

**TIP:**
*For good bhaturas, put them in medium hot oil and do not touch for a few seconds till they rise a little. Press the edges lightly till they puff up and then turn. Fry till very light golden.*

**NUTRITIONAL VALUES** (per portion): Energy 339 cal, Protein 6.5 gm, Carbohydrate 40.0 gm, Fat 17 gm

# CHUTNEYS & PICKLES
# RAITAS & SALADS

India being a hot country, yogurt is relished at all the meals. Raita is yogurt seasoned usually with spices like roasted ground cumin or ground black salt along with some herbs. Besides this, there are many unusual ways of flavouring yogurt. Raitas can also be served as a dip or a sauce with side dishes. Always use plain yogurt for preparing any 'raita'. Chutneys are popular with an Indian meal. These are thick flavourful sauces which perk up the meals. Salads are not traditional but have now become a part of Indian meals.

# CABBAGE & COCONUT SALAD

*Serves 4*

*South Indians love coconut in all their dishes. The brown skin of the coconut kernel should be removed before grating the coconut for this salad. A combination of red and green cabbage may be used to make the salad more interesting.*

## INGREDIENTS

- 125 g/4 oz plain yogurt (½ cup)
- 1½ cups shredded cabbage
- ½ cup freshly grated coconut
- 1 tsp finely grated ginger
- 2 green chillies - deseeded & chopped, optional
- salt to taste

### TEMPERING

- 2 tbsp oil
- ½ tsp mustard seeds *(sarson)*
- ½ tsp cumin seeds *(jeera)*
- a pinch of red chilli powder

## METHOD

1. Whisk yogurt. Keep it in a large mixing bowl. Toss cabbage, coconut, ginger, green chillies in the yogurt. Add salt to taste. Keep aside.

2. Heat 2 tbsp oil, reduce heat. Add cumin seeds and mustard seeds. When they pop and stop crackling, remove from heat. Add a pinch of red chilli powder and pour over the prepared salad. Mix lightly. Serve.

**NUTRITIONAL VALUES** (per portion). Energy 35.63 cal, Protein 2.09 gm, Carbohydrate 3.81 gm, Fat 1.31 gm

# RAITA ANAARKALI

*Serves 4*

*A sweet and sour raita with fresh kernels of pomegranate. Slices of boiled potatoes are arranged around the yogurt. The tamarind chutney is very simple to prepare and it can be stored for many days in the freezer. You may have this raita even without the tamarind chutney.*

## INGREDIENTS

- 500 g/1 lb plain yogurt (2 cups)
- 1 cup fresh pomegranate kernels - *(anaar daana)*
- ½ tsp red chilli powder
- ½ tsp salt or to taste
- 1 tsp ground, roasted cumin *(bhuna jeera)*
- 2 small potatoes - boiled and cut into slices
- a few fresh coriander leaves - to garnish
- 1 tbsp tamarind *(imli)* chutney

### TAMARIND (IMLI) CHUTNEY

- 1 tbsp tamarind pulp
- 3 tbsp sugar, or to taste
- ½ cup water
- ½ tsp ground ginger *(optional)*
- ¼ tsp black salt
- salt or to taste
- ½ tsp ground, roasted cumin *(bhuna jeera)*

## METHOD

1. Mix all ingredients of the tamarind chutney. Keep on heat and stir well to mix. Cook till a saucy consistency is reached. Cool. The chutney will thicken as it cools.

2. Beat the yogurt well till absolutely smooth. Add the pomegranate kernels, salt, cumin seeds and red chilli powder to the beaten yogurt. Transfer to a flat serving dish. Surround the dish with boiled potato rounds.

3. Pour a little chutney on the potato slices. Arrange a small bunch of whole coriander leaves in the centre. Garnish with kernels of pomegranate.

**NUTRITIONAL VALUES** (per portion): Energy 256 cal, Protein 4.25 gm, Carbohydrate 20.5 gm, Fat 5.05 gm

# HARI CHUTNEY

*Serves 4*

*A green chutney prepared front fresh coriander and mint leaves. As long as this chutney is there with my meals, I can enjoy anything without creating a fuss. My favourite!*

## INGREDIENTS

- ½ cup mint leaves (pudina leaves)
- 1 cup fresh coriander (hara dhaniya) - chopped along with stems
- 2 green chillies
- 1 onion - chopped (½ cup)
- ½ tsp dried mango powder (amchoor)
- ½ tsp sugar
- ½ tsp salt

## METHOD

1. Wash coriander and mint leaves. Grind all the ingredients together to a smooth paste. Serve with snacks or with meals.

**NUTRITIONAL VALUES** (per portion): Energy 19.13 cal, Protein 1.62 gm, Carbohydrate 2.71 gm, Fat 0.20 gm

# PUDINA RAITA

*Serves 4*

*This is one of the most popular form of yogurt in summers. The cooling effect of mint helps to keep us cool during the scorching heat of summers. If you like, you may do without the chopped onions and tomatoes. I like them for the crunch which they add to the yogurt.*

## INGREDIENTS

- 500 g/1 lb plain yogurt (2 cups)
- ¾ cup chopped mint leaves (pudina)
- 1 tsp powdered sugar
- 1 tbsp raisins (kishmish)
- ½ onion - chopped finely (¼ cup)
- 1 tomato - chopped finely (¼ cup)
- 1 green chilli - chopped finely
- salt and red chilli powder to taste

## METHOD

1. Whisk yogurt well, till smooth. Wash mint leaves well and grind to a rough paste.
2. Add mint paste and all the ingredients to the yogurt. Mix well. Keep in the fridge till serving time.

**NUTRITIONAL VALUES** (per portion): Energy 111.75 cal, Protein 7.15 gm, Carbohydrate 8.70 gm, Fat 5.40 gm

# COCONUT & PEANUT CHUTNEY

*Serves 6*

*This authentic chutney, originating from Southern India, is superb with all types of bean and lentil appetizers. Fresh coconut is traditional, but to make the procedure simpler, you may opt for the desiccated coconut instead.*

## INGREDIENTS

- ½ cup freshly grated or desiccated coconut
- ½ cup roasted peanuts (without the red skin)
- 1 green chilli - chopped
- 1 onion - chopped (½ cup)
- ½ tsp salt, or to taste
- ½ inch/1 cm piece ginger
- 1 cup yogurt - approx.

### TEMPERING

- 1 tbsp oil
- 1 tsp mustard seeds *(sarson)*
- 1-2 dry, red chillies - broken into bits
- a few curry leaves

## METHOD

1. Grind all ingredients of the chutney adding enough curd to get a thick paste of soft dropping consistency. Keep aside in a bowl.

2. To temper the chutney, heat 1 tbsp oil. Add mustard seeds. When they splutter, add broken red chillies and curry leaves. Remove from heat and pour the tempered oil on the chutney. Mix lightly.

**NUTRITIONAL VALUES** (per portion): Energy 287.63 cal, Protein 9.35 gm, Carbohydrate 10.65 gm, Fat 12.31 gm

# CUCUMBER AND DILL RAITA

*Serves 4*

*A lovely combination of greens - cucumber and dill in yogurt, makes a perfect accompaniment to any meal. The freshly ground coarse peppercorns enhance the taste.*

## INGREDIENTS

- 500 g/1 lb plain yogurt (2 cups)
- ¾ cup thickly grated unpeeled cucumber
- 1 tsp powdered sugar
- ½ tbsp dried dill flakes
- ½ tsp peppercorns - coarsely ground
- salt to taste

## METHOD

1. Whisk yogurt well till smooth. Grate thick shreds of a small unpeeled cucumber on the grater.

2. Add all the ingredients to the yogurt. Mix well and transfer to a serving bowl. Sprinkle some dill flakes on top. Keep in the fridge till serving time.

**NUTRITIONAL VALUES** (per portion): Energy 79.88 cal, Protein 4.03 gm, Carbohydrate 4.69 gm, Fat 5.04 gm

# SWEET MUSHROOM PICKLE

*Makes 500 g/1 lb*

*A very interesting sweet and sour pickle with fresh mushrooms.*

## INGREDIENTS

- 500 g/1 lb button mushrooms
- 50 g/2 oz (1 pod) garlic - ground to a paste
- 2 inch/5 cm piece ginger - ground to a paste
- ¾ cup oil
- a pinch of asafoetida (hing)
- 4 tsp red chilli powder
- 5 tsp mustard (rai) powder
- 5 tsp salt
- ½ cup raisins (kishmish)

### GRIND TOGETHER

- 2 tsp fenugreek seeds (methi dana)
- 2 tsp sesame seeds (til)

### BOIL TOGETHER

- 1 cup vinegar
- 3-4 tbsp ground jaggery (gur)

## METHOD

1. Boil 4-5 cups water with 2 tsp salt. Add mushrooms and boil for about 5 minutes till a little soft. Drain & dry on muslin cloth for 5-6 hours.

2. Heat oil in a kadhai or a deep pan. Fry the garlic paste till light golden, then add ginger and fry till golden brown. Add asafoetida. Add the ground sesame and fenugreek seeds. Remove from heat. Add red chilli powder, ground mustard and salt. Mix the mushrooms with this masala.

3. In a pan heat vinegar. Add jaggery & cook on low heat till jaggery dissolves. Remove from heat and add kishmish.

4. Add to the mushrooms. Mix well. Put in a jar. Consume within 2 weeks or refrigerate if it has to be kept for a longer period.

**NUTRITIONAL VALUES** (per portion): Energy 126.88 cal, Protein 0.93 gm, Carbohydrate 1.82 gm, Fat 12.70 gm

# GARLIC PICKLE

*Makes 500 g/1 lb*

*A very easy pickle to prepare. It helps in also digesting the food besides adding zest to the food.*

## INGREDIENTS

- ½ kg garlic - peeled
- ½ cup mustard oil
- ½ cup vinegar
- 25 gm (5 tsp) salt
- 2 tsp ground turmeric (haldi)
- 4 tsp red chilli powder
- 4 tsp ground mustard (rai powder)

## METHOD

1. Peel the garlic. Heat mustard oil to smoking point. Reduce heat. Add all the garlic together. Cook for 2 minutes on low heat. Let it cool.

2. Heat vinegar in a separate pan. Remove from heat. Add salt, turmeric, red chilli powder and ground mustard.

3. Mix the garlic in oil to the masalas in vinegar. Fill it in dry bottles. This pickle can be eaten immediately also.

**NUTRITIONAL VALUES** (per portion): Energy 81.25 cal, Protein 1.58 gm, Carbohydrate 7.45 gm, Fat 5.03 gm

# DESSERTS & SWEETS

Our prized spices — saffron from Kashmir and green cardamoms from South India, are generally used in flavouring Indian desserts. Saffron imparts a lovely yellow colour as well as a delicate flavour to the dessert. Pistachios and almonds are used generously in sweets to add the much desired crunch, whereas silver leaves and rose petals enhance the visual appeal of Indian sweets.

# KESAR KULFI FALOODA

*Serves 6-8*

*The delicious Indian Ice cream topped with sweetened thin vermicelli. Saffron lends it's flavour and colour to this most popular Indian dessert. Pistachios and almonds add to the richness.*

## INGREDIENTS

- 1 litre/1 quart (5 cups) milk
- 5 tbsp skimmed milk powder
- 3 tbsp cornflour
- 1/3 cup sugar, or to taste
- 6-7 strands saffron *(kesar)*
- 3-4 green cardamoms *(chhoti elaichi)* - crushed
- 1 tbsp shredded pistachios *(pista)*
- 1 tbsp shredded almonds *(badam)*

### FALOODA

- 1 cup thin rice vermicelli
- 3-4 strands saffron *(kesar)*
- 3 tbsp sugar
- 2 green cardamoms *(chhoti elaichi)*

## METHOD

1. Dissolve cornflour and milk powder in ½ cup milk to a paste. Keep aside.
2. Boil rest of the milk with sugar and saffron. Simmer on low heat, for about 15 minutes till slightly thick.
3. Add the paste gradually, stirring continuously. Mix well. Add crushed seeds of green cardamoms. Boil. Simmer for 4-5 minutes. Remove from fire.
4. Cool. Add pistachios and almonds. Fill in clean kulfi moulds and leave to set in the freezer for 6-8 hours or overnight.
5. To prepare the falooda boil 4 cups water. Add the rice vermicelli. Boil. Simmer on low heat for 2-3 minutes till the vermicelli turns soft and no crunch remains. Strain. Add cold water to refresh. Strain again.
6. Make a sugar syrup by boiling ¾ cup water, 3 tbsp sugar, saffron and green cardamoms together. Simmer for a couple of minutes. Remove from heat and put in the boiled vermicelli. Keep soaked in sugar syrup, in the refrigerator, till serving time.
7. To serve, remove the kulfi from the mould, cut into two halves lengthways and top with some falooda (without the syrup). Serve.

Step 2

Step 4

**NUTRITIONAL VALUES** (per portion): Energy 95.61 cal, Protein 4.22 gm, Carbohydrate 16.72 gm, Fat 0.18 gm

# GAJAR KA HALWA

*Almost every home in India has a box stocked with this carrot pudding in winters. It is served hot during the cold winter months, when fresh, red carrots are in plenty.*

## INGREDIENTS

- 500 g/1 lb carrots - grated into long shreds
- 1 cup milk
- ¼ cup sugar
- 2-3 tbsp ghee or unsalted butter
- 5-6 almonds (badam) - shredded
- 10-12 raisins (kishmish)
- seeds of 3 green cardamoms (elaichi) - crushed

## METHOD

1. Boil milk with crushed cardamom seeds in a clean wok or a deep pan. Add grated carrots & cook uncovered, stirring occasionally, till milk dries.
2. Add almonds and raisins. Stir for 1 minute. Add sugar. Cook till the mixture turns dry again.
3. Add ghee and stir fry for 10 minutes on low heat till ghee separates. Serve hot garnished with some nuts.

**NUTRITIONAL VALUES** (per portion): Energy 240.46 cal, Protein 1.94 gm, Carbohydrate 32.17 gm, Fat 11.57 gm

# KALAKAND

*For this great delicacy, milk has to be curdled in a special way so that it does not separate fully; it should just form tiny granules. If you add too much tartaric acid, the milk curdles fully and the greenish water separates. This makes the cheese hard and chewy. The mixture should be milky (whitish) in colour and semi-dry when removed from fire. If you dry the mixture too much and then set, it becomes like milk cake.*

## INGREDIENTS
- 1 litre/1 quart (5 cups) full cream milk
- 3-4 pinches tartaric acid, about 1/8 tsp
- 2 tsp cornflour
- 80 gm sugar (1/3 cup)
- 4 green cardamom seeds - powdered
- 4 pistas - chopped

## METHOD
1. Boil milk in a kadhai. Add tartaric acid pinch by pinch till the milk curdles slightly. Very tiny granules should stick at the back of the spoon. The milk does not curdle fully and there is no green whey seen.
2. Add sugar. Keep boiling on high flame, stirring constantly. Boil for about 18-20 minutes till the mixture thickens. Reduce heat. When the mixture becomes semi-solid & frothy sprinkle cornflour over it. Stir for 2-3 minutes.
3. Turn the mixture onto a greased tray/box. Spread a 1½" thick even layer in a tray. Decorate with cardamoms and pista. Let it set for 2-3 hours. Do not refrigerate. Cut into squares. Store in the refrigerator.

**NUTRITIONAL VALUES** (per portion): Energy 278 cal, Protein 15.2 gm, Carbohydrate 35.1 gm, Fat 9.0 gm

# BESAN LADDOO

*Gramflour, ghee and sugar – simple ingredients that are transformed in carefully controlled steps to make a complex little bomb of taste explosion.*

## INGREDIENTS
- 100 gm gramflour (*besan*)
- 20 gm semolina (*suji*)
- 100 gm castor sugar
- 50 gm ghee
- a pinch of turmeric (*haldi*)
- ¼ tsp powdered cardamom

## METHOD
1. Heat ghee in a kadhai.
2. Add gramflour and semolina to ghee and mix well. Keep stirring so that no lumps form. Continue frying till fragrant and light brown in colour.
3. Remove from fire. Add turmeric and mix well. Spread in a plate to cool slightly.
4. Add castor sugar and mix.
5. Add powdered cardamom and shape into round balls while still hot.

**NUTRITIONAL VALUES** (per portion): Energy 121 cal, Protein 1.6 gm, Carbohydrate 14 gm, Fat 6.5 gm

# PHIRNI

*A milk pudding cooked with ground rice paste and flavoured with saffron and green cardamoms.*

## INGREDIENTS

- 4 cups milk
- 1/3 cup basmati rice or rice flour
- 1/3 cup sugar, or to taste
- 4-6 almonds *(badam)* - shredded
- 5-6 pistachios *(pista)* - shredded
- 2 small silver leaves, optional
- seeds of 2-3 green cardamoms *(elaichi)* - powdered
- a few strands saffron, to garnish, optional
- a few crimson rose petals for garnishing

## METHOD

1. Soak rice for about an hour and then grind it very fine with 4 to 5 tablespoons of water to get a paste. (Rice flour may be used as a substitute). Dissolve the rice paste or rice flour in some milk and make it thin of a pouring consistency.

2. Mix the rice paste with the milk in a heavy bottomed pan. Cook on medium heat, stirring continuously, till the mixture is of a creamy consistency.

3. Add sugar and cardamom powder and stir. Simmer for 4-5 minutes till sugar is fully dissolved.

4. Remove from heat and add half of the shredded almonds and pistachios.

5. Pour the mixture into 6 small bowls. Let it cool to room temperature.

6. Decorate each bowl with a silver leaf and a few shredded nuts. Arrange a rose petal. Serve chilled.

Step 2

Step 5

**NUTRITIONAL VALUES** (per portion): Energy 239 cal, Protein 4.13 gm, Carbohydrate 22.5 gm, Fat 5.46 gm

# MAKHANE KI KHEER

*Serves 8-10*

*Milk is cooked with roasted lotus seeds to a creamy consistency. Cardamom enhances the flavour.*

## INGREDIENTS

- 2 litres/2 quarts full cream milk
- 100 gm lotus seeds (*makhane*) - roast for 1-2 minutes in a pan
- ¾ cup sugar or to taste
- ½ tsp green cardamom (*elaichi*) powder
- 2-3 tbsp screwpine flower (*kewra*) water, or a drop of extract
- 1 tbsp chopped green pistachios
- silver leaf to decorate

## METHOD

1. Roast the lotus seeds in a flat pan, stirring continuously, till they start to change colour. Let them cool. Crush half of them, leaving the other half whole.
2. Boil milk. When the milk starts to boil, add the lotus seeds and cook in milk on medium heat, stirring every now and then. Cook till the lotus seeds are cooked and the consistency of the milk reduced by one third.
3. Add sugar and sprinkle crushed cardamom. Cook further for a couple of minutes. Remove from heat.
4. Add kewra water. Transfer to a serving dish. Decorate with silver leaf and chopped pistachios.

**NUTRITIONAL VALUES** (per portion): Energy 338 cal, Protein 5.9 gm, Carbohydrate 35 gm, Fat 6.58 gm

# KADDU KA HALWA

*Makes 12*

*Here is a halwa that starts with the humble vegetable, pumpkin. It is lifted to the highest level of elegance with ingredients like poppy seeds, saffron, almonds, khoya and raisins. Yes, it deserves the garnish of silver leaf, pistachio and rose petals!*

## INGREDIENTS

- 2 kg/4 lb yellow pumpkin (*kaddu*)
- 8 tbsp poppy seeds (*khus khus*)
- ½ cup sugar, or to taste
- seeds of 6-8 green cardamoms (*elaichi*)
- 1 tbsp saffron (*kesar*) - dissolve in 1 tbsp hot water
- ½ cup ghee
- 250-300 gm khoya - grated
- 2 tbsp chopped almonds
- 2 tbsp raisins (*kishmish*)

## GARNISH

- a silver leaf (*vark*)
- a few green pistachios - blanched and sliced
- a few rose petals

## METHOD

1. Peel and chop pumpkin into small pieces.
2. Clean and wash the poppy seeds well.
3. Place the pumpkin in a pressure cooker with ¼ cup water and give 2 whistles, remove from heat.
4. Place the cooked pumpkin in a kadhai and mash it with the back of a laddle. Add the poppy seeds, crushed cardamom seeds and saffron. Cook on medium heat till water evaporates and the pumpkin turns dry.
5. Add sugar and stir till dry. Cook, stirring for 5 more minutes.
6. Add ghee and cook for 10 minutes on low heat to get a rich brown colour.
7. Add the khoya, raisins and almonds. Mix well.
8. Serve hot garnished with silver leaf, pistachios and rose petals.

**NUTRITIONAL VALUES** (per portion): Energy 226 cal, Protein 6.08 gm, Carbohydrate 20.8 gm, Fat 13.08 gm

# international conversion guide

*These are not exact equivalents; they've been rounded-off to make measuring easier.*

## WEIGHTS & MEASURES

| METRIC | IMPERIAL |
|---|---|
| 15 g | ½ oz |
| 30 g | 1 oz |
| 60 g | 2 oz |
| 90 g | 3 oz |
| 125 g | 4 oz (¼ lb) |
| 155 g | 5 oz |
| 185 g | 6 oz |
| 220 g | 7 oz |
| 250 g | 8 oz (½ lb) |
| 280 g | 9 oz |
| 315 g | 10 oz |
| 345 g | 11 oz |
| 375 g | 12 oz (¾ lb) |
| 410 g | 13 oz |
| 440 g | 14 oz |
| 470 g | 15 oz |
| 500 g | 16 oz (1 lb) |
| 750 g | 24 oz (1 ½ lb) |
| 1 kg | 30 oz (2 lb) |

## LIQUID MEASURES

| METRIC | IMPERIAL |
|---|---|
| 30 ml | 1 fluid oz |
| 60 ml | 2 fluid oz |
| 100 ml | 3 fluid oz |
| 125 ml | 4 fluid oz |
| 150 ml | 5 fluid oz (¼ pint/1 gill) |
| 190 ml | 6 fluid oz |
| 250 ml | 8 fluid oz |
| 300 ml | 10 fluid oz (½ pint) |
| 500 ml | 16 fluid oz |
| 600 ml | 20 fluid oz (1 pint) |
| 1000 ml | 1¾ pints |

## CUPS & SPOON MEASURES

| METRIC | IMPERIAL |
|---|---|
| 1 ml | ¼ tsp |
| 2 ml | ½ tsp |
| 5 ml | 1 tsp |
| 15 ml | 1 tbsp |
| 60 ml | ¼ cup |
| 125 ml | ½ cup |
| 250 ml | 1 cup |

## HELPFUL MEASURES

| METRIC | IMPERIAL |
|---|---|
| 3 mm | 1/8 in |
| 6 mm | ¼ in |
| 1 cm | ½ in |
| 2 cm | ¾ in |
| 2.5 cm | 1 in |
| 5 cm | 2 in |
| 6 cm | 2½ in |
| 8 cm | 3 in |
| 10 cm | 4 in |
| 13 cm | 5 in |
| 15 cm | 6 in |
| 18 cm | 7 in |
| 20 cm | 8 in |
| 23 cm | 9 in |
| 25 cm | 10 in |
| 28 cm | 11 in |
| 30 cm | 12 in (1 ft) |

## HOW TO MEASURE

When using the graduated metric measuring cups, it is important to shake the dry ingredients loosely into the required cup. Do not tap the cup on the table, or pack the ingredients into the cup unless otherwise directed. Level top of cup with a knife. When using graduated metric measuring spoons, level top of spoon with a knife. When measuring liquids in the jug, place jug on a flat surface, check for accuracy at eye level.

## OVEN TEMPERATURE

*These oven temperatures are only a guide. Always check the manufacturer's manual.*

| | °C (*Celsius*) | °F (*Fahrenheit*) | Gas Mark |
|---|---|---|---|
| Very Low | 120 | 250 | 1 |
| Low | 150 | 300 | 2 |
| Moderately Low | 160 | 325 | 3 |
| Moderate | 180 | 350 | 4 |
| Moderately High | 190 | 375 | 5 |
| High | 200 | 400 | 6 |
| Very High | 230 | 450 | 7 |